The Thing I Miss Most is My Mind

Endorsements

The endorsements below are from preeminent leaders, experts, and scholars in the fields of neurology, neuroscience, dementia, and Alzheimer's research and clinical practice, as well as other prominent professionals who are active in supporting Alzheimer's research, education, and caregiving services:

> I have read the chapters you sent and want you to know how very excited I am about your upcoming book on Alzheimer's disease. You've successfully combined scintillating first-person narratives, up-to-date insights from leaders in the field and sound practical advice for persons and caregivers dealing with this disease. I have never read anything quite like it before. Given that there are over 5 million people in the US suffering from Alzheimer's disease, almost everyone is touched by this illness nowadays. Your book will fill a niche in the Alzheimer's literature, and I foresee a large audience of potential readers. When families of Alzheimer's patients come to my office, they frequently ask me what they should read to learn more about this illness. I very much look forward to being able to recommend your book to them for that purpose. Congratulations!
>
> —Norman R. Relkin, MD, PhD,
> Associate Professor of Clinical Neurology and Neuroscience, and Director, Weill Cornell Memory Disorders Program, Weill Cornell Medical College, NewYork-Presbyterian/Weill Cornell Medical Center

This book is written with the same inquisitive mind that Bettye demonstrated as a student nurse at Duke. It is a wake-up call as Alzheimer's will touch all of us either emotionally or financially. It is a threat to our health care system and our society. This is a guide with the information needed for one to think about necessary decisions. Bettye had a tragic journey but triumphed with this book as a positive way to help others.

—William G. Anlyan, MD, Chancellor Emeritus, Duke University Medical Center

The human brain is a universe unto itself with a hundred billion neurons and quadrillions of synapses making up the neural networks that bring you your own personal world. Bettye Musham's book highlights this amazing organ at its best and its very worst, as in Alzheimer's disease, which "robs" a person of one's very self. We will beat brain diseases like Alzheimer's through "early prediction–early detection–early prevention." In the meantime, we desperately need books like this that provide practical advice on what to do when this "thief of self" enters into your world. This accessible book addresses these timely issues and more in a uniquely informed, compassionate and practical way.

—Rudolph E. Tanzi, PhD, Joseph P. and Rose F. Kennedy Professor of Neurology, Harvard University Director of the Genetics and Aging Research Unit, Massachusetts General Hospital

Alzheimer's continues to grow as a major disease, taking family and friends away from us in a long and drawn-out process. Bettye Marlin Musham's book helps bring the disease to light in a personal way that touches the heart and soul.

—Alexandra Lebenthal, President and CEO, Lebenthal Holdings, LLC

The Thing I Miss Most is My Mind

An Insider's Guide to Achieving Positive Results When Confronting Alzheimer's

Bettye Martin Musham

FEDORA PRESS

Copyright © 2019 by Bettye Martin Musham

All Rights Reserved. Except as permitted under the U.S. Copyright act of 1976, no part of this publication may be reproduced, distributed, or transmitted in any form or by any means, or stored in a database or retrieval system, without the prior written permission of the publisher.

First Edition January 2019

Learn more about the author or this publication at: www.fedorapress.com

Author photo by Saul Leiter

ISBN: 978-1-936712-08-3

Published in the United States of America

DISCLAIMER: *The publisher, FEDORA PRESS, will not be held responsible for the contents of this book. Every effort possible was made to secure permission from Professor Sy Moskowitz for the use of his quotes.*

Contents

Endorsements 3
Foreword 9
Introduction 13
Remembering 15

1: Why This Book? 17

2: A Love Story 20
    How We Met 20

3: Transitions 24
    From Happiness and Good Health to Harassment and Hard Decisions 24

4: Understanding the Stages of Alzheimer's Disease 38
    The Process of Retrogenesis 38

5: Legal and Financial Matters 78
    The Importance of Being Well-Informed and Well Organized 78

6: Arranging for Proper Care 95
    An Introduction from a 95
    Caregiver's Perspective—What It Feels Like When You Have a Primary Caregiver's Role and Responsibility 95

7: Taking Care of the Caregiver 128
    Put On Your Own Oxygen Mask First 128

8: Death 154
    Rediscovering and Recovering Your Self and Picking Up the Pieces of Your Own Life 154
    Glossary of Alzheimer's Disease Terms 162
    Acknowledgments 178
    About the Author 179

Foreword

There are many books about Alzheimer's disease, covering the gamut of issues related to the devastating loss of a loved one, the burdens of caregiving, and the long and progressive nightmare of the insidious illness. Most of these narratives tell stories of an individual or a family and reveal how the disease has torn people apart or brought them together. Some of these books are practical handbooks for caregivers. But few books are comprehensive as a single source, and many are simply not interesting to read. The experience of living with the illness is so individual that, despite common themes, the experience itself becomes the best teacher. Here, however, is an Alzheimer's book that tells a life story, and an interesting one at that.

The book resonates with my experience as a geriatrician who has cared for thousands of people with Alzheimer's over the past thirty-five years. I generally see people toward the end of their lives, but it is their rich life story that makes my work so interesting. I may, for example, see an eighty-year-old man and his wife of sixty years. They have been through incredible struggles, successes, and failures. They have had children and grandchildren and through all their ups and downs, they have survived, even flourished, across almost a century. Their experiences span from a time when there was no internet or even television, from a time of great war, and from the Depression. And now they are in my office. The man has memory problems, and both are really scared. And unlike the "old days" (just twenty or thirty years ago) when Alzheimer's was either locked away in the closet or utterly unheard of, the couple has not only heard of Alzheimer's, but they have seen it affect their friends and loved ones. They know what it is, what to expect, and where it will take them. So, what is my job? It is to celebrate their lives, to do a life review, and to see how we got here. It is to reassure them life is not over, that it will go on, and that I will help care for them through this time of fear and loss. That is my role as a physician: to care for people who are sick. And people with Alzheimer's disease are certainly sick. Indeed, Alzheimer's is a chronic, progressive, uniformly fatal neurodegenerative disease.

So, what is different about this book? It tells the story of an extraordinary couple in an honest and compelling way. And it has the geriatrician's perspective woven throughout. It discusses where we have been in our understanding of this devastating disease, how we got here, and where we are going. It describes real people with real pitfalls and flaws, moving through life in the best way they know how— people who have resources, access, and success but, despite all this, experience real struggles. Struggles that reach across all strata of our society. There are lawsuits, divorces, love and romance, joyous moments, and disastrous times.

And then Alzheimer's happens. One day, something is noticed. It's subtle; it's nuanced; it's not really there, or if it's there, it's not quite believable. If it is believable, then it must be denied. It can't be. And from this denial come guilt, recriminations, conversations, and accusations about what could have been done differently.

Now children, family members, friends, lawyers, and trustees are engaged in financial abuse of a cognitively frail, vulnerable elder. Financial management of once-significant assets falls apart. A previously robust, brilliant, independent, autonomous man must be supervised. The privileges that are taken for granted by all adults are removed, and autonomy is lost. There is rage and defense and resistance and finally, surrender.

Caregiving in all its forms walks in through the door. Normal life is in chaos. Lost forever, gone, never to return. The technical aspects of Alzheimer's care become the priority, but the emotional impact of watching a loved one disappear is wrenching. There is a dual need to bond and rebond and yet also an urge to separate, to preserve one's self, to begin to move on while the loved one is still there, at least in body if not in mind.

This Alzheimer's book is different because it combines passion with practicality. It combines the personal experience of a life well-lived, through the phase of Alzheimer's, with a comprehensive technical perspective on Alzheimer's care. It pulls no punches and it doesn't avoid an exploration of the ugly side of Alzheimer's. There are chapters on how to protect yourself from the wolves of family members who want Dad to change the will when Dad can't remember his birth date or how old he is, as well as chapters on human sexuality in institutional settings.

The book is written for the lay person, but it will be useful for doctors and nurses and other health care providers. It needs to be on everyone's bookshelf and read by those who are committed to making the life of a person with Alzheimer's a life of quality.

In the end, there is only one way out of the nightmare and that is to end Alzheimer's, to discover and develop new drugs that prevent the onslaught of cognitive decline and dementia, which is becoming the greatest epidemic of the developed world in the twenty-first century. We must do this so that older persons can live productive lives well into late old age, contributing their wisdom, experience, and knowledge to their families, friends, and society.

They deserve to see a peaceful end of their lives, one without suffering.

—Howard Fillet, MD, Founding
Executive Director and Chief Science Officer,
Alzheimer's Drug Discovery Foundation

Introduction

This is a personal love story of a journey from falling in love, marriage, and happiness, to watching your loved one disappear in stages over time. I deal with the progress of the disease from the vague beginning of symptoms that one does not know clearly how to label to the end of life.

This book follows the many phases of the disease from when you and your loved one are struggling together, to finding out what is wrong and what can be done, to the gradual shift to the one who must face the decisions for caring.

Each couple arrives at this moment with different histories of decision-making, between the two and within the family. As symptoms differ from person to person and may be complicated due to other ongoing medical problems, this is the most difficult and trying phase of early detection of the disease.

Finding a competent source of medical advice is essential. Many medical centers do not have a group that deals only with the problems of aging and that have access to staff that can perform the various medical and psychological testing that is necessary. Only once this testing is completed can the other problems be dealt with, problems that relate to the care and advice that are necessary to maintain one's dignity and meet one's financial and legal needs.

I have tried to outline the path of the disease that I experienced, which seems to be more or less what generally occurs, as well as offer information that I believe will help others confronted by the dilemma of how to cope with Alzheimer's disease. When I confronted the situation, I felt a lack of adequate advice on what the problem was and engaged in a search for answers. I could not find one resource that outlined what I was experiencing, what I might be facing as the disease progressed, and where I could find help. It took weeks of reading and talking with various kinds of doctors to finally reach a pragmatic path to a probable diagnosis.

I say "probable diagnosis," because Alzheimer's disease can be confirmed only after death, with an autopsy.

Remembering

When my grandfather immigrated to the United States from China fifteen years ago, he developed a daily routine of going through a box of old family photos. At the beginning, he provided each photo with a lively anecdote for anyone to hear. After a few short years, he began to shift through the box in solitude, with hardly any acknowledgment of surrounding company. Little did I know, his practice of going through the images was more than just the pastime of a sentimental old man; it was the effort of a man longing to remember his past while trying to reconcile his reality.

My grandfather was diagnosed with Alzheimer's disease at the age of seventy-six, but signs of dementia were apparent long beforehand. As his health deteriorated, family members took turns taking care of him, some more willing and ready than others. Though, regardless of how one steps into the role of the caregiver, the responsibilities and emotional tolls of taking care of a loved one with Alzheimer's remain the same. I hope the financial and legal planning tools in this book will provide some guidance and comfort to readers and caregivers everywhere.

I would like to extend a very special thank you to Ms. Bettye Martin Musham, for allowing me to contribute to this project. I would also like to thank my parents and sister, whose courage and grace through difficult times have consistently shown me that compassion has no limit.

—Julia Cheung, Esq., BA, Johns Hopkins University; MA, Columbia University; JD/LLM, Duke University School of Law

Why This Book?

In its own way, this book is designed as a guidebook that can provide you with the keys to organizing your personal journey into caregiving and navigating the labyrinth of both the legal and health care systems in this country. This book has been born out of my own intense personal experience of having been an Alzheimer's disease caregiver, in addition to the experiences of countless others, so that you can better help your own loved ones through this difficult stage of life. These chapters are meant to provide you with a practical roadmap to guide your steps in coping with the expected and the unexpected challenges of Alzheimer's disease.

Dr. Rudolph E. Tanzi, a Harvard neuroscientist, and Ann B. Parson, in their groundbreaking book *Decoding Darkness: The Search for the Genetic Causes of Alzheimer's Disease* (2001) writes that few real nightmares on earth compare to the terror wrought by Alzheimer's disease. Its initial symptoms of forgetfulness and personality change lie so close to normalcy that they typically go unnoticed, and once noticed, too long unexplained.

Alzheimer's disease is no respecter of persons. Some of the most prominent, brilliant, and creative minds of recent history have been affected, including top world leaders in business, science, medicine, law, education, politics, sports, the media, and the arts.

Like a threatening tornado, Alzheimer's disease may strike those closest to home and dearest to us—husbands and wives, mothers and fathers, sisters and brothers, grandparents and adult children, aunts and uncles, friends and lovers—leaving widespread devastation in its wake. It is true that with recent advances in brain imaging technology, medical science has been making great strides in understanding the possible causes and progression of the disease. Although medications, such as Aricept, may provide some relief in suppressing symptoms for a period of time, Alzheimer's still has no known cure.

As you begin your search to find the best medical attention and care for your loved one at risk for or suffering from dementia, I want to share some important information for your consideration. In 2018, the direct cost to our society of caring for those with Alzheimer's disease and other dementias will total $277 billion.

According to Harry Johns, president and CEO of the Alzheimer's Association, urgent, meaningful action is necessary, particularly as more and more people age into greater risk for developing a disease that has no cure and no way to slow or stop its progression. Estimates indicate that by 2050, the number of people sixty-five and older with Alzheimer's disease will reach 13.8 million and could reach as high as 16 million people. One in three seniors dies with Alzheimer's disease or another form of dementia.

While these figures for Alzheimer's sufferers are alarming enough, they do not include family members and caregivers, who also suffer untold financial, physical, and emotional stress from trying to cope with and manage their loved one's situation. As of 2012, 15.4 million caregivers gave 17.5 billion hours of unpaid care. The monetary cost of unpaid caregiving services alone is already estimated at more than $216 billion per year. And, this staggering figure does not begin to include the costs of medical care, pharmaceutical expenses, paid in-home and institutional care, or community and respite services—all of which threaten to overwhelm an already-fragile economy and overburdened health care system.

There are a number of other realities that we are now facing when it comes to the growing incidence of this potentially catastrophic epidemic:

- One in nine people, over age sixty-five, have Alzheimer's disease.

- Two-thirds of Americans with Alzheimer's are women.

1. Why This Book?

- Every sixty-eight seconds, someone in the United States develops Alzheimer's disease. By the middle of the twenty-first century, this will happen every thirty-three seconds.

- Alzheimer's disease is the third leading cause of death in the United States, after heart disease and cancer, according to a March 2014 *New York Times* editorial, up from the sixth leading cause, as was previously thought.

While research into the causes of this disease is ongoing and in-depth, there is still no cure. For further information, go to: www.alz.org/search facts & figures.

Against such a mind-numbing statistical backdrop, loving, caring, and concerned people like you are desperate for answers and are not sure where to go or whom to turn to for advice and to get help when they need it most.

This book begins with my story of deep love and personal caregiving and contains a treasure trove of practical advice, professional and community resources, and shared experience in dealing with the myriad aspects of Alzheimer's care.

The information that follows is by one who has "been there and done that." I hope that you will find this book and the resources it contains helpful, as you walk with your loved one through the dark valley, in the long shadow of Alzheimer's disease.

And, despite the truly daunting challenges you are now facing, it is my greatest hope that you may also find moments of joy and love along the way.

2

A Love Story

How We Met

In 1978, I was in the midst of a divorce and trying to raise a teenage child on my own. I also had recently started my own business, which required a good bit of travel and burning the midnight oil. My company was beginning to take off, so I was constantly on the go pursuing business connections and networking with colleagues. Yet, despite my hectic work schedule, I managed to spend quality time with my daughter and keep in touch with old friends. Little did I know the surprise I was in for at the next event on my social calendar.

It was an invitation to a New York dinner party, except it was not the usual set of circumstances. Leila Hadley was an acquaintance of many years, as we both worked in the fashion and the advertising business. She came from the Blue Book society circle, twice divorced with three beautiful children that I used as models whenever an opportune moment arose. Leila had an interesting group of friends, so her parties were fun. Charles Adams, the cartoonist, was always in attendance, as well as names from the society columns.

Leila had recently married a man from Chicago. She was giving a party to introduce the new husband to the New York gang. Most of the parties brought together writers, artists, and such. I agreed to come and bring my friend. The party was crowded, but, as I knew most of the people, it was easy to include the new husband, Bill Musham, in several of the conversations. Shortly after our

2. A Love Story

arrival, I said good night and left with my Indiana boyfriend.

The following morning, I had a six a.m. flight to Chicago for a business meeting and from there, I planned to go to Las Vegas for a trade show. My new business was GEAR Holding, Inc. As cash was scarce, I was flying economy class. The airline overbooked the flight, and I was moved to a first-class in a seat next to Bill Musham. He said if I was going to be in Chicago overnight, he would invite me to dinner and gave me his number to call. When I missed my flight to Las Vegas, I had dinner with Bill Musham. We talked all night, until my early morning flight. The next day in Las Vegas, I received a call from Bill saying he was coming to Las Vegas to finish our conversation. As his wife, Leila, was off to India for a visit of undetermined time, that became the beginning of my love story with Bill Musham, who would later become my husband and greatest friend.

As you can imagine, life was not easy for many months after that first encounter. I was in the midst of a very nasty divorce from a doctor who did not want to grant it. Nevertheless, Bill and I were together from then on, despite the problems it presented for his eventual divorce. When Leila returned two months later without having sent Bill a single letter during her absence, he, too, asked for a divorce. Eighteen months later, Bill was granted a divorce from Leila and we were married.

No one knows the exact role that stress plays in inducing Alzheimer's; however, most physicians attribute ongoing and severe stress as the gateway for many diseases. Stress is the root of many physical and emotional problems. The part of the brain that determines which hormones to release and when to release them is called the amygdala. Chronic repetitive stress disables the natural body response to stress, which enables the amygdala to release stress hormones. From the time Leila returned from India and was presented with divorce papers, she was a constant source of stress—phone calls to me, phone calls to Bill, and her lawyer calling my housekeeper, my husband that I was divorcing, and our common friends. Day and night she persisted in an attempt to stop the divorce.

Bill's unfortunate marriage to Leila had occurred at the end of a series of other traumatic events in Bill's life. His former wife was dying of breast cancer; the company he had transformed from his grandfather's foundry to a top-ranking international industrial company traded on the New York Stock Exchange was the target of a hostile takeover; and he was in the midst of a major international acquisition. When his wife died in 1975, he was introduced to Leila by Darrell Ruttenberg, a close business friend, and Bill soon became a target acquisition for Leila. They were married the same year. Their three-year marriage presented, according to Bill, a new level of stress and a tortured relationship.

Stress and the Onset of Alzheimer's: Grappling with an Insidious Gremlin

Stress is difficult; it has different meanings in different contexts. There is good stress, which can often lead to higher achievement and bad stress, which can trigger disease and even lead to untimely death. According to the American Institute for Stress, "While everyone can't agree on a definition of stress, all of our experimental and clinical research confirms that the sense of having little or no control is always distressful—and that's what stress is all about."

In a relaxation mode, the body can heal itself. One can reprogram the subconscious mind to aid the body in self-healing to deal with stress. Simple ways to relax, like sitting quietly for ten to twenty minutes a day (meditating) can help anyone cope with adversity. To drive away the stress gremlin it is best to find ways to combat loneliness, if loneliness is the problem. Acts of generosity always make someone feel better, as does interaction with others. The internet, today, affords the opportunity to find other people or groups that share one's interests.

Life Was Sweet: Before Alzheimer's

After the ordeal of both of the divorces and the sweetness of finally becoming man and wife, Bill and I both relished the opportunity to be happy together. I had an apartment in Venice for many years, as well as a home in Marbella, Spain. Now, we had the time and peace of mind to visit Italy and Spain. Bill had never visited either country, so it was especially exciting to introduce him to new places and to my friends.

Life was so wonderful with Bill. He was seventeen years older than I, played tennis most days and golf on the weekends, flew his own plane, was very active as vice chairman of Gould, Inc., in addition to being a member of many corporate boards. He was handsome and loving and planned our life to be full of intellectual pursuits, travel, and interesting friends. We studied at Oxford during the summer, took sailing vacations, hiked in Scotland, went sculling on the Delaware, and retreated to the Bucks County farm that we both loved. Life was sweet—before Alzheimer's.

Our Bucks County farm was ideal. The farm is eighty-five acres of woods, surrounding the ten acres we claimed for our house. The 1870s barn we had converted in 1980 to a guest house provided housing for family and friends. The tennis court and swimming pool were all we needed to make life very pleasant for us and our many house guests and friends.

In 1985, Bill retired from Gould, Inc., where he was vice chairman, and from the boards of Walgreens, Corestates Bank, and Carson Prie Scott. He retired from all the other boards he served on when he reached their mandatory retirement age.

This was difficult for Bill, as he was accustomed to a very active business life and creating wealth by joint ventures with foreign companies. He sought other avenues for his talents, for example, creating a program at Marymount Manhattan College, which was next to our townhouse in Manhattan. The program was designed for people over fifty and was called the Center for Living and Learning. It brought needed funds to the college and proved a magnet for students and faculty within the neighborhood and beyond. Older people wanted to learn, and many proved to be great teachers.

At the same time, Bill joined a similar program in Doylestown, Pennsylvania, at the Bucks County Community College. Both were modeled after the Harvard University program for older people to continue to learn and teach. I believe that all these activities delayed the onset of Bill's symptoms of Alzheimer's for many years.

3

Transitions

From Happiness and Good Health to Harassment and Hard Decisions

There were many subtle warnings that I should have noticed as unusual and considered as perhaps the start of Alzheimer's disease. Bill's medical issues started with knee-replacement surgery in 1983 and went on to prostrate surgery in 1984. Then a tumor was removed from his thigh in 1985, and in 1986, the original knee replacement was replaced. The surgeries were associated with frightening apprehension and disorientation for Bill. He started testing himself to be sure his mind was working. When hospitalized, he was so worried that he would call me several times a day, even during the night, to reassure himself that he could remember our telephone number. These post-surgical experiences would pass after several days. I don't know if these episodes were related to early symptoms of Alzheimer's disease, but they were out of character for this self-assured, confident, and fearless man.

We continued to travel and entertain. Then, in 1995, I became increasingly concerned about Bill's state of mind. He loved parties, and to celebrate his eightieth birthday, we planned a very special party with friends and relatives from out of town.

It is wonderful to remember all the small loving moments that Bill and I shared in the early years of our life together amid the stress of our business lives

3. Transitions

and court appearances for each of our divorces. Every Wednesday evening, wherever we were, we would talk over our weekend plans. It always involved a flight, to somewhere, for one of us in the early days. Whenever possible, if Bill had to be in Europe or Asia, I would accompany him. The anticipation of being together never left. The strong intimacy and bond between us endured. To look into Bill's blue eyes and see the love returned was magical. To see the dimming of the same blue eyes was heartbreaking. Bill always wanted to go to sleep at night with me curled around his back. This was a comfort to him, even as the disease progressed and his sleep was fitful. We both welcomed the warmth of a loved one's body.

Watching someone you love deteriorate is very lonely. The gradual descent, from the onset through various stages to the end, is filled with many mixed emotions. Guilt that you should have done more. Relief that both of you can now stop. Overwhelming tiredness. Your body aches, your mind aches, and your heart aches. It is almost as if you had stopped being yourself, too, because of numbness that fills your body and soul. It takes a while to comprehend the experience.

It was in 1995 that I should have known something was significantly wrong, but I made excuses to myself. All the little signs were there. Burned tea kettles, burnt toast, water left running in the kitchen until the well in our country house ran dry. It seemed every time Bill was at the farm alone something would go awry. I said to myself that it was the pain killers he was taking to ease the knee pain until surgery could be scheduled. The pain killers were part of the problem but not all of it. I decided to arrange for friends to go to the farm if I could not go on the same day as Bill. Socially, Bill was still the same person, but now, this easy-going, very intelligent man seemed distracted. He had always tried to learn five new words every day from his reading. One day, I noticed that the index cards on which he wrote each word were missing.

After being forced to acknowledge that this was a bigger problem than I had previously thought, I realized the question now was to find out what exactly the problem was. My husband was surrounded by doctors continuously: a cardiologist, an orthopedist, an internist, a rheumatologist, and a dermatologist. He was so intelligent, active, well read, curious about life, and enthusiastic, I never gave aging or diseases associated with aging any consideration. Calls to his existing doctors resulted in a consensus: we should wait until after the upcoming knee surgery and then start decreasing his pain medication. This jogged my brain, forcing me to recall Bill's previous surgeries and the disorientation he experienced afterward. I began to worry and dissect what was really happening to him.

I had graduated from Duke University's School of Nursing and kept up with my acquaintances and old friends from there over the years. I called Duke University's chancellor of the medical center, Dr. Bill Anlyan, who put me in contact with Dr. Robert Rowe, who was then the head of Mt. Sinai Hospital in Manhattan. Dr. Rowe had organized what was widely recognized as one of the foremost geriatric practices in the United States. Bill was scheduled for testing. He would undergo a comprehensive neurological evaluation as well as a neuropsychology test. He was now eighty years old and looked much younger. The doctors reviewed his numerous medications and examined him as a whole person and not a collection of parts. They did brain scans to see if he had had small strokes that would not show up in a routine MRI. They also administered tests to determine if his brain was functioning correctly. When he did not perform very well on these tests, they gave him more to see if he had had a stroke and look for any other discernible causes for the poor performance of his mind. Bill did his best to mask the problems, but the diagnosis was the same: in all likelihood, Bill was undergoing early-onset Alzheimer's disease.

We were referred to Dr. Norman Relkin at New York Hospital, who proved to be a godsend. The hard decisions that had to be made were now becoming apparent. For one, should we label the disease or not? Bill refused to accept the fact that there was a problem. He recalled that when he had had a small tumor removed from his leg, he had been disoriented for some time, and this, he insisted, was just a similar episode.

To label or not label a disease as devastating as Alzheimer's is an emotionally challenging decision. Bill became very hostile at the mere mention of his having Alzheimer's disease. I decided not to press the issue but began taking steps to protect him. It is a conflicting time in early-stage Alzheimer's, because the symptoms come and go. At times, he would be perfectly attuned to many aspects of our daily life, but then suddenly and without notice, he would change to the point where he was unable to comprehend even simple situations. He had been a wonderful navigator whenever we traveled by car, but now he often found directions to familiar places puzzling.

There developed a pattern of small things that were not normal but not too abnormal either. For instance, when we ate out, Bill would ask me to tally up the tip, explaining that I was more generous, so I should determine the tip amount. It soon dawned upon me that he could not add the numbers. This was a big wake-up call, as he had once been practically a genius with numbers and, to everyone's amazement, had used a slide rule rather than a calculator. He managed our stock portfolio on a daily basis, so I was faced with the challenge of how to investigate this without alarming him. We paid bills from the farm on weekends with the assistance of a local person who would write the checks after Bill looked over the invoices. All of a sudden, alarm bells were ringing all over.

Irregularities included bills being paid twice or bills entirely overlooked. Financial planning that had previously taken only a few hours now turned into work for the entire weekend. As I began to try to help with the financial tasks Bill had always done so easily, I became aware of other problems. Our long-term housekeeper, who also helped Bill with preparing checks for his signature, filing papers, and so on, had been steadily increasing her wages and even paying herself in duplicate. I had previous discussed with her some of the problems Bill was confronting and asked her to help in being more observant.

Little did I know that someone—a long-trusted person whom we paid above-average wages and helped to deal with some of her own financial and marital problems—was taking advantage of Bill in this situation. I began to look closely at our checkbook and discovered that several checks to an unknown entity, totaling $100,000 over a few days, had been cashed. This prompted me to ask our bank how I could remove Bill's name from our joint checking account. Surprisingly enough, only when I discussed the checks with Bill, did I discover how much more was at stake.

Mood Swings: Bellwether of Impending Storms

Mood swings usually increase as the disease progresses and as the sufferer becomes aware of what is happening. The awareness that one is disappearing and not able to control one's own life is very frightening.

Bill was always a very even-tempered person and never one to criticize others; he would always put forth his suggestions in a very positive way. Early on, however, I began to notice his personality change. For example, he was, at times, cruel.

Once, when we were vacationing at Round Hill in Jamaica, he started interrupting conversations with fellow guests with comments that were hostile. When I suggested that we should dine alone, he would suggest that I was ashamed of him and asked why. He would have no memory of this afterward. Then again, at times, he would question the fact that he was not able to be of help to me or to himself. This usually happened after the financial advisors would visit to review our portfolios.

On one occasion, upset at his failing to be of help to me or himself, Bill expressed the desire to kill himself. I would not discuss this with him and said this was a matter he should discuss with his priest. The priest, Father Boniface Ramsey, would visit Bill most Thursday evenings and share a bottle of wine. I mentioned this to Boniface, but Bill never brought it up with him. He was delighted to have Boniface visit and it seemed to comfort him.

Bill could become very aggressive at times with the physical therapist and the occupational therapist, even lashing out to hit them. This was so out of character for Bill that it was alarming. Finally, they refused to come, as Bill would not comply with their instructions, and the striking was completely unacceptable. It became my job to do the regular exercise routine with Bill, as well as supervise the occupational therapy exercises. All this was to keep Bill in good physical health so he could take his own showers, shave, dress himself, and walk independently.

It seems people with Alzheimer's often experience something called sundowning, in which, as the evening goes on, the sense of reality decreases. This symptom occurs in most people with Alzheimer's, and it happens at the

3. Transitions

time of day when most caregivers are fatigued. Sundowning involves the slowing down of mental function and physical energy in an Alzheimer's patient toward the end of the day, usually around dusk—hence, the sunset-related term. The cause of this phenomenon is not entirely understood, but many physicians speculate that, due to the stress on the person's entire neurological processing system, at this point in the body's circadian cycle, the Alzheimer's patient has totally exhausted his or her reserves due to the great efforts expended just to cope with the most basic tasks of existence.

We were able to recruit caregivers from folks at our church to stay with Bill during the day, along with our in-house help, and hired a male aide, recommended by the Alzheimer's service to stay with him at night. Since this disease takes away the ability to determine day from night, Bill would often want to take a walk during the night. New York doormen are some of the kindest people in the world. Before we were able to secure a night person, when Bill would appear in his pajamas at the front door of the lobby, our doorman would engage him in conversation and assist him back to our apartment, after calling me. The uncertainty of not knowing whom a loved one could encounter in a situation like this is very distressing to those who are responsible for primary care.

Mealtimes were also a challenge. At times as Bill would not remember if he had had a meal or whether that meal was breakfast, lunch, or dinner. As diet and exercise are so important in maintaining one's ability to be self-sufficient, this kind of memory lapse presents quite a dilemma. He would often ask for a cocktail at breakfast time. "Why can't I have a martini?" was a frequent question.

Keeping the same, familiar caregivers around is important, as no one knows for certain what degree of awareness the person suffering with Alzheimer's is experiencing. In caring for a loved one with Alzheimer's, it is also important to keep the person occupied. Bill liked to play backgammon, bridge, and chess and to read. He often played the games incorrectly but with enough resemblance to the game to pass. Books on tape were good entertainment and offered a wide variety of titles. Friends came for lunches and walks. In the various stages of Alzheimer's and other dementias, for the sufferer to be able to take a walk on his or her own is not to be taken for granted. The time period from having a modicum of personal mobility to not being able to get around independently at all differs greatly between individuals.

Bill did not take to the idea that someone had to go with him to take a walk. I had tried to postpone the need for him to be accompanied on his walks by ensuring that Bill always had his address in his wallet and enough money in easy-to-calculate denominations—such as one- and five-dollar bills, for taxi fares. It seems that many taxi drivers are used to older people and are helpful and patient in getting them to the right address and making sure that the payment is correct.

In addition to compassionate people and kind strangers, pets also seem to be a comfort to those with Alzheimer's. So much is unknown about this disease, but this aspect is widely acknowledged. Although we did not have a dog in New York, Bill was overjoyed when friends would come with their pets. Bill would hold the dog in his arms and would not want to let it go. As the disease progressed, it became obvious that pets were of great importance to my husband.

New Cognition and Memory Tests: How Bill Finally Accepted His Diagnosis of Alzheimer's

The possibility that he had Alzheimer's disease was abhorrent to Bill. He would not discuss it with me or any one of the people we relied on for advice, such as the people at our bank, our attorney, and so on. Visits to neurologists, whose waiting rooms were filled with people suffering from Alzheimer's and whose examinations were totally related to memory questions did not convince Bill he had memory problems. Finally, I ordered from Johns Hopkins Medical Center their twenty-two white papers on Alzheimer's disease, hypertension, and arthritis. I left them in our library and Bill began reading them. We never discussed the diagnosis, but after that, Bill objected less to having someone with him most of the time.

3. Transitions

Alzheimer's at Home and on the Go: Safety, Transportation, and Wandering Issues—Making Life Safer and Travel Easier for a Person with Dementia

Dementia is no one's fault, but it also knows no boundaries. Someone who is cognitively impaired is not necessarily going to be aware of danger to him- or herself or others. As a person with Alzheimer's loses mental clarity and becomes increasingly restless and/or disoriented, families must face important issues of safety and wandering so that they and the caregivers can keep their loved ones with dementia safe and secure.

At Home: Safety Proofing the Living Environment
It is up to the primary caregiver and other family members to make sure that the environment is not fraught with dangers, either obvious or hidden. Kitchens and bathrooms are common sites of most home accidents.

In the kitchen, cleaning supplies and small home appliances, such as microwave ovens and electric mixers, must be secured in an inaccessible area. Storage cabinets, both above and below counter level, should also be locked. Knobs on gas ranges should be removed when not in use. Treasured collectibles should be taken off shelves.

In the bathroom, you may need to install grab bars and tamper-proof locks on cabinets, windows, and closet doors. Medicine cabinets are especially dangerous for dementia patients and accidental ingestion of medications must be prevented. Hair dryers, shaving equipment, and hair-treatment supplies, for example, must be maintained out of sight and out of reach.

Throughout the entire house, electrical outlets and wiring need to be hidden or sheathed. Extra lighting should be installed in hallways and stairwells, and treads should be put on stairs. Rugs and carpets should be removed or taped down so that someone who is easily distracted won't trip. Since Alzheimer's patients have a tendency to wander, all exits and windows to the outside need to be locked securely.

Other areas that can pose potential danger for a person with Alzheimer's include the basement and garage, pool house, and any barns or other outbuildings. Common items that must be secured under lock and key or other reliable means include carpentry tools, gardening equipment, cleaning supplies, and dangerous machinery; packing crates, steamer trunks and other luggage; animal cages, pet carriers, fish tanks, and terrariums; step-ladders, chains, barbed wire, and ropes; paint cans, lacquers, spray paints, and painting solvents; glues, grout, cement, and roofing tar; pesticides, anti-freeze, gasoline, kerosene, lighter fluid, plumbing chemicals, and other toxic agents; and sports, exercise, camping, and other recreational gear.

Moreover, laundry facilities, irons, ironing boards, clothes lines, and drying racks, must be made inaccessible, as should lawn-maintenance equipment and hobby supplies; bicycles, skate boards, snow skis, and ice skates; canoes and kayaks; jet skis, fishing, and boating paraphernalia; and any appliances, such as meat slicers, freezers, refrigerators, ranges, barbecue units, and ice makers. Finally, all motorized tools and motor vehicles should be deactivated and/or stored securely and be inaccessible to one with Alzheimer's.

The residential building itself may harbor safety hazards for someone with Alzheimer's. Handrails and ramps may be necessary. If the house has stairs, elevated decks, or attic windows, a person with slightly compromised perception or full-blown dementia may fall or get hurt trying to escape from an upper room. A backyard swimming pool is another area in which accidents frequently occur. Draining and professional sealing may be required. Playground equipment, barns, and agricultural equipment can also present dangers to those who are dementia-compromised.

Admittedly, this list is not definitive. If you have dangerous items or know of any perilous structural challenges in the residence of your loved one, it is incumbent upon you to make sure that these situations are remedied or at least that the person with Alzheimer's is kept out of harm's way. Due diligence must be performed to protect a cognitively impaired person.

3. Transitions

Danger on the Road

Bill, Driving, and Alzheimer's

As a primary caregiver, you may find yourself responsible not only for ensuring that your Alzheimer's-impaired one is safe at home, but also that he or she will be safe in transit.

With Bill, driving was a big issue of contention. He had been an excellent driver and had even piloted his own plane, so the idea of not driving was a huge affront.

His failing to observe traffic signs—in addition to his forgetting how to locate familiar places—was the signal to me that I had to somehow stop Bill from driving. Many people who are older confuse the brake and gas pedals, an all too common situation that often results in traffic accidents.

It is important for us to confront this difficult safety issue, while at the same time, bear in mind

that giving up driving entails feelings about the loss of independence. Driving is a complex activity that requires quick thinking and reactions, as well as good perceptual abilities. For the person with Alzheimer's disease, driving becomes a safety issue. While he or she may not recognize that changes in cognitive and sensory skills impair driving abilities, you and other family members will need to be firm in your efforts to prevent the person from driving when the time comes for the individual's safety, as well as others'. Some states require a physician to report a diagnosis of Alzheimer's disease to the Health Department, which sends it on to the Department of Motor Vehicles. In the meantime, you can make your own personal assessment by taking note of any signs of unsafe driving.

The loss of independence can be devastating to anyone. It is, however, especially important for someone with Alzheimer's disease, to be reassured that there will be alternative transportation available. Obtaining the person's voluntary cooperation in giving up driving and easing that transition period are important tasks for you, the person's caregiver, as well as for the person's entire family and circle of friends.

One way of reinforcing the no-driving policy is by asking your physician to advise that driving is no longer permitted for medical reasons, or to write a letter or prescription stating that the person with Alzheimer's disease must not drive.

To discourage people with dementia from driving, you can start by reducing their need to drive. Medications, groceries, and meals can be delivered. You, or other family members, can offer to chauffeur your loved one to and from appointments. Or, if this presents a burden at times, you may be able to enlist the help of organizations in your community. For example, many places of worship coordinate member volunteers to drive people who are no longer able to drive themselves. You can also arrange for a taxi service or sign up for a special transportation service available only to older or disabled people. Another suggestion to deter one with dementia from driving is to substitute a photo ID card for the person's driver's license.

Try to dissuade the person from driving by pointing out that someone else should drive for various reasons: because it's a new route or there's bad traffic—use your imagination! If you are driving, it might be a good idea for someone else to sit in the backseat for distraction, especially if the person with Alzheimer's has a tendency to become angry or aggressive. As a caregiver, you cannot take any chances with this issue.

You should pursue all avenues to ensure that your dementia-impaired person does not become a safety hazard to him- or herself or to anyone else by trying to drive. If the person with Alzheimer's refuses to stop driving, here are a few tactics of last resort:

- Hide the car keys. Provide a set of fake keys that look like the real set but don't work.

- Disable the car by removing the distributor cap, battery, or starter wire. Install a system to prevent ignition turnover unless a switch is thrown.

- Have the person's license revoked by the Department of Motor Vehicles

- This may require documentation from a physician, certifying

3. Transitions

that the person has Alzheimer's disease; is a hazard on the road, and is no longer able to operate a vehicle.

Traveling

Traveling requires advanced planning to ensure a safe and pleasurable trip for all. After determining the stage of the person with dementia, one of the first things you should consider before your trip is enrolling the patient in MedicAlert® +Alzheimer's Association Safe Return®, if the person is not already enrolled. If the person is enrolled, notify the program of your travel plans.

When in the planning phase of your trip, be sure to consider your patient's needs. For instance: is there a specific time of day your patient is at his or her best? You may want to plan your travel time accordingly. Getting to your destination should be short and simple; try not to travel during peak seasons or times.

The two most commonly used methods of transportation are automobiles and airplanes.

- If you are traveling by car, try to bring another person with you, preferably someone who can share the driving and who can also help with your patient.

- Make sure you have emergency equipment (spare tire, jumper cables, flashlight, water, and so on) in the car you'll be traveling in.

- Bring your traveler's favorite books and music with you to help pass the time.

- Make sure to schedule rest stops and bathroom breaks every couple of hours.

- If you are traveling by airplane, schedule as few layovers and flight changes as possible.

- Take advantage of TSA Cares (855-787-2227), a free help line designed to assist travelers with disabilities and medical conditions, prior to getting to the airport.

- Travelers are encouraged to call TSA Cares seventy-two hours before traveling, with questions about screening policies and procedures and to learn what to expect at security checkpoints.

- When you get to the airport, speak with airline personnel about how they can best assist you and your traveler. Since dementia is often a nonapparent disability, you may want to bring a note from your traveler's physician.

- Airports are very busy places, and taking advantage of the airline's escort services may be helpful. Request a wheelchair so you and your traveler can be given priority at security checkpoints, airport gates, and during the boarding process.

- Be sure to also remove items which may cause your traveler to set off the metal detector. Have him or her wear slip-on shoes to make the shoe-removal process easier during security checks.

Whether traveling by car or airplane, the following tips can be helpful:

- Encourage your traveler to dress in clothes that are comfortable and easy to put on and remove.

- Include a card with his or her name and the contact information of the place where you will be staying.

- Have medications, insurance cards, physician's information, an extra set of clothing, and snacks in a small travel bag.

- It would be best to give some background about your traveler's condition to the relatives you will stay with, in advance of your arrival.

- If your plans include a gathering, suggest an open house in which other family members and guests can drop in and leave

3. Transitions

at different times, since people with dementia usually do better with just a few guests at a time.

- Give your family members suggestions on how they can best interact with your traveler, as you are the best judge of what your traveler can or cannot tolerate and may or may not enjoy.

- Once you arrive at your destination, call the Alzheimer's Association's twenty-four-hour help line at 800-272-3900 for information about the local chapter at your destination.

Understanding the Stages of Alzheimer's Disease

The Process of Retrogenesis

During the downward-spiraling trajectory, there are certain definable stages in the relentless progression of Alzheimer's disease. In the first, there are no symptoms whatsoever. Then, evidence of mild cognitive impairment appears, often sporadically, so it's quite mystifying to everyone involved. As the disease advances, one finds increased memory loss, spatial disorientation, general confusion, and personality change. Over the course of four to eight years from diagnosis, on average, the disease progresses to moderate cognitive impairment and finally to severe dementia, with its concomitant loss of identity and bodily control. In the final and fatal stage, a person with Alzheimer's disease loses consciousness and continence, as well as the ability to swallow and even to breathe. New York University neurologist Barry Reisberg has concluded that Alzheimer's disease unravels the brain almost exactly in the reverse order that it develops from birth. He calls this process retrogenesis.

In his insightful and poignant book, *The Forgetting: Alzheimer's: Portrait of an Epidemic*, David Shenk recounts how the scientific connection between the childlike nature of Alzheimer's dementia and the course of neurological development in normal children came about:

4. Understanding the Stages of Alzheimer's Disease

New York University neurologist Barry Reisberg realized that the Alzheimer's-childhood analogy is not just anecdotal—that it could be measured scientifically. Reisberg was a pioneer in defining stages and substages of Alzheimer's, trying to gain a much more precise understanding of the disease's trajectory. The more he drilled down on the exact order of abilities lost, the more he was impressed by the comparison to child development. He began to notice that there were precise inverse relationships between stages of Alzheimer's disease and phases of child development in the areas of cognition, coordination, language, feeding, and behavior. He documented these observations in comparison charts. Placed side by side, the sequences of abilities gained and lost nearly perfectly mirror one another. In neurological exams, there were similarly precise inverse relationships in EEG activity, brain glucose metabolism, and neurologic reflexes. The only possible conclusion Reisberg could draw was that, like the winding and unwinding of a giant ball of string, Alzheimer's unravels the brain almost exactly in the reverse order as it develops from birth. . . . Reisberg called it "retrogenesis"—back to birth.

The Adapted FAST: Introduction and Application

Experts have documented common patterns of symptom progression that occur in many individuals with Alzheimer's disease and developed several methods of "staging" based on these patterns.

Staging systems provide useful frames of reference for understanding how the disease may unfold and for making future plans. But, it is important to note that not everyone will experience the same symptoms or progress at the same rate.

Within this framework, I have noted which stages correspond to the widely used concepts of mild, moderate, moderately severe, and severe

Alzheimer's disease. I have also noted which stages fall within the more general divisions of early-stage, mid-stage, and late-stage categories. However, each person's experiences are different. The Adapted FAST identifies the stages as follows.

Stage 1

- No impairment (normal function)
- Unimpaired individuals experience no memory problems and none are evident to a health care professional during a medical interview.

Stage 2

- Very mild cognitive decline (may be normal age-related changes or earliest signs of Alzheimer's disease)
- Individuals may feel they have memory lapses, especially in forgetting familiar words or names or the location of keys, eyeglasses, or other everyday objects. But, these problems are not evident during a medical examination or apparent to friends, family, or co-workers.

Stage 3

Mild cognitive decline

- (early-stage Alzheimer's disease—can be diagnosed in some, but not all, individuals with symptoms)
- Friends, family, or co-workers begin to notice deficiencies.
- Problems with memory or concentration may be measurable in clinical testing or discernible during a detailed medical interview.

4. Understanding the Stages of Alzheimer's Disease

Common difficulties include the following:

- Problems finding words or names
- Decreased ability to remember names when introduced to new people
- Performance issues in social or work settings noticeable to family, friends or co-workers
- Retaining little material after reading a passage
- Losing or misplacing a valuable object
- Decline in ability to plan or organize

Stage 4

- Moderate cognitive decline (mild, or early-stage, Alzheimer's disease)
- Decreased knowledge of recent occasions or current events
- Impaired ability to perform challenging mental arithmetic, for example, to count backward from seventy-five by sevens
- Decreased capacity to perform complex tasks, such as planning dinner for guests, paying bills, and managing finances
- Reduced memory of personal history
- Subdued and withdrawn demeanor, especially in socially or mentally challenging situations

Stage 5

- Moderately severe cognitive decline (moderate, or mid-stage, Alzheimer's disease)
- Major gaps in memory and deficits in cognitive function emerge. Some assistance with day-to-day activities becomes essential.

- Inability during a medical interview to recall such important details as current address, telephone number, or the name of the college or high school from which they graduated
- Confusion about where they are or about the date, day of the week, or season
- Trouble with less challenging mental arithmetic, for example, counting backward from forty by fours or from twenty by twos
- Needing help choosing proper clothing for the season or the occasion
- Usually retaining substantial knowledge about themselves and knowing their own names and the names of their spouse or children
- Usually requiring no assistance with eating or using the toilet

Stage 6

- Severe cognitive decline (moderately severe, or mid-stage, Alzheimer's disease)

Memory difficulties continue to worsen, significant personality changes may emerge, and affected individuals need extensive help with customary daily activities. At this stage, individuals may

- Lose most awareness of recent experiences and events as well as of their surroundings
- Recollect their personal history imperfectly, although they generally recall their own name
- Occasionally forget the name of their spouse or primary caregiver but generally can distinguish familiar from unfamiliar faces
- Need help getting dressed properly; without supervision, may

4. Understanding the Stages of Alzheimer's Disease

  make such errors as putting pajamas over daytime clothes or shoes on wrong feet

- Experience disruption of their normal sleep/waking cycle

- Need help with handling details of toileting (flushing toilet, wiping and disposing of tissue properly)

- Have increasing episodes of urinary or fecal incontinence

- Experience significant personality changes and behavioral symptoms, including suspiciousness and delusions, for example, believing that their caregiver is an impostor; hallucinations (seeing or hearing things that are not really there); or compulsive, repetitive behaviors such as hand-wringing or tissue shredding

- Tend to wander and become lost

Stage 7

- Very severe cognitive decline (severe, or late-stage, Alzheimer's disease)

This is the final stage of the disease when individuals lose the ability to respond to their environment, the ability to speak, and, ultimately, the ability to control movement.

- Frequently individuals lose their capacity for recognizable speech, although words or phrases may occasionally be uttered.

- Individuals need help with eating and toileting and there is general incontinence of urine.

- Individuals lose the ability to walk without assistance, then the ability to sit without support, the ability to smile, and the ability to hold their head up. Reflexes become abnormal and muscles grow rigid. Swallowing is impaired.

In order to assess the progression of your loved one's dementia, the adapted FAST might be administered by a physician, who will interview you by asking questions about your loved one's behavior and/or by watching the person engage in activity. The description that best fits the person's performance may be the stage in which the person is functioning.

Enhancing Brain Health: Lifestyle Changes in Diet, Exercise, and Sleep Habits That Can Make a Difference

Alzheimer's disease has not been described as an epidemic. Although it is not communicable in the same sense as infectious diseases, Alzheimer's disease, nevertheless, poses a great public health threat. One of the reasons for this widespread threat is that we have no drugs to combat the disease itself, only medication to mask its symptoms for a limited period of time.

Yet, according to Dr. Norman Relkin, director of the Memory Disorders Program at NewYork-Presbyterian/Weill Cornell Medical Center in New York City, over the past several years there has been a ten to 15 percent decrease in the number of new Alzheimer's cases reported in the United States, annually. This is most likely due to the development of new drugs to control hypertension (high blood pressure) and diabetes. These two diseases appear to be the most prevalent doors to Alzheimer's, so if we can keep them at bay, perhaps we can put a roadblock in front of Alzheimer's disease.

Among other precipitating factors, oxidative stress, inflammation, and depression are also frequently associated with the onset of Alzheimer's. Reducing these known triggers by maintaining a healthy lifestyle may be more than just a popular celebrity pastime. According to many health care professionals, it may very well be an essential key to defeating the dragon of Alzheimer's. To this end, some of the most promising research today is focused on detecting Alzheimer's early enough to keep those with the highest risk for Alzheimer's disease well.

Until only recently, people have ignored the importance of maintaining brain health. In fact, they have often taken their brains for granted. When decades of unhealthy habits begin to exact an inevitable toll, these folks are not

4. Understanding the Stages of Alzheimer's Disease

only taken by surprise but actually shocked. For instance, many athletic coaches and the institutions that support their teams have, heretofore, turned a blind eye to the long-term effects of concussions on the brain health of their players. Only now, after so many retired athletes have begun to report symptoms of Parkinson's disease and other neurological disorders, have colleges, universities, and sports franchises finally begun to wake up to the long-term threat to brain function posed by multiple concussions in the boxing ring, football field, and/or hockey rink.

And only recently has a small segment of the general public begun to realize how important what you eat and how you exercise are to long-term brain functioning. In light of the irrefutable correlations between diet and exercise habits and brain health, this is not enough. More people must become aware of the impacts of their own lifestyle choices on cognition, well-being, and aging.

It seems that at this point, we need a public-health intervention that could alert people to the need of staying well through exercise, diet, and remaining mentally active and socially engaged into advanced old age. This idea is not such a radical concept as it may at first appear. As a nation, we have initiated successful public-health interventions in the past to fight tuberculosis, polio, and HIV-AIDS, as well as a number of previously rampant childhood diseases, such as measles, mumps, chicken pox, diphtheria, whooping cough, and rubella. And now, considering the number of people who are diagnosed with Alzheimer's disease, the number who are at-risk, and the financial impact this disease alone has on our health care costs, it is now critical that the medical establishment, the government, and the media join together to intervene on behalf of aging and early-onset adults to raise greater public awareness of Alzheimer's and what people can do to prevent it.

A federal and state initiative, tied to corporate America, urging workers to participate in diet and exercise programs would be a step forward. Physical education in our schools needs to be seen as a necessary part of wellness in general and brain health in particular.

In another arena, the widely publicized trial of Brooke Astor's son, prosecuted by Manhattan's elder-abuse assistant district attorney, Elizabeth Loewy, was helpful to this cause because, despite its unseemly aspects, this high-profile court case made a larger number of people more aware of Alzheimer's disease, its ultimate impact on brain health, and the toll it takes on families.

Why do we find it so hard to do simple things that make our life worth living? Most of us find multiple excuses not to exercise or eat a healthy diet; however, faced with the fact that we are responsible for the health of our brain and our heart and the commensurate consequences if we don't take care of them, who wouldn't sit up and take note? You would think everyone would, right? Yet, this is far from the reality, as a quick look around will confirm—obesity, diabetes, chronic obstructive pulmonary disorder (COPD), heart disease, stroke—these diseases are running rampant in our aging Western societies.

When it comes to Alzheimer's disease—now considered the third major cause of death in the United States, we can take positive steps to maintain brain health and possibly postpone the symptoms, even if we can't postpone the disease itself. As we age, many of us develop a variety of ailments, which can improve with our taking care of our brain and our heart.

No one has found the magic bullet to stop Alzheimer's disease. Neurologists have explained that the disease gums up the brain with protein clumps and tangles. But, it's not just clumps and tangles. Damage to the brain's blood vessels—often due to high blood pressure, smoking, or diabetes—can also play a role, and not just in dementia but also in milder memory loss as well. When it comes to implementing positive lifestyle changes that will affect the health of the brain, it's never too soon to make brain-healthy choices. The disease takes root in the brain twenty to thirty years before a diagnosis is ever made, and although the average age of diagnosis is in the early seventies, it's important to start protecting one's brain much earlier.

First of all, we should eliminate smoking. The nicotine in cigarettes causes the blood vessels to constrict, thereby raising blood pressure and inhibiting blood flow to the whole body, including the brain. We should also practice good habits to ensure brain safety, such as wearing a helmet when bicycling or participating in strenuous contact sports. Even small concussions can have long-term effects, some of which predispose a person to Parkinson's disease, Alzheimer's, and other forms of dementia.

It is not unusual for people with dementia to have mixed health problems. When the arteries become stiffened and narrowed, it is much harder for the blood to flow normally. This can lead to a stroke, something 20 percent of older people experience without being aware of it. Even a mini-stroke—transient ischemic attack (TIA) or silent cerebral infarct (SCI)—can contribute to mild cognitive memory problems.

When we ask how to enhance brain health, we cannot forget one important factor: the heart. There is an important connection between the heart and the brain, as Dr. Tanzi reminds us in *Decoding Darkness*. He specifically states that accumulating studies provide evidence of a heart-brain connection in Alzheimer's disease. What's bad for the heart appears to be bad for the brain—which should surprise no one. How the two are related is undergoing rigorous examination. Possibly, past generations were not that far off in thinking that hardening of the arteries does hasten dementia by permitting amyloid buildup. Dr. Tanzi also states that there's reason to expect that a good cardiovascular flow has a detoxifying effect on the brain.

So, knowing how to keep your brain working for as long as possible means simply this: when you're doing the right thing for your heart, you're also helping your brain. Maintaining brain health requires basic good health goals for a heart-friendly diet and ongoing exercise, as well as stimulating mental activity. Other controllable factors include managing blood pressure and blood sugar levels and getting enough sleep.

Of course, when probable Alzheimer's is the diagnosis, not all health factors are controllable. But, by diligently shoring up the ones that are responsive to health-enhancing interventions and lifestyle changes, we, as caregivers, can help our loved ones enjoy the brain function they still have, for as long as possible. And we ourselves can benefit from paying attention to our own health habits as well. In the ensuing paragraphs, we will look at some of the controllable factors in maintaining and enhancing brain health.

Blood Pressure and Vascular Disease

Monitoring your blood pressure can reduce the risk of late-life cognitive impairment. High blood pressure drives vascular disease, which may result in small strokes and a higher risk of developing Alzheimer's. It's become fairly clear cut, maintains Mike Mullan at the University of South Florida, that "if a person is predisposed toward vascular problems, it can bring out Alzheimer's and that Alzheimer's in turn can bring out vascular irregularities."

Some researchers have called Alzheimer's a form of vascular disease. In a lecture that I attended, one of the preeminent voices in Alzheimer's research, Dr. Sidney Strickland, president of Rockefeller University, spoke about his studies on how blood flow and clot formation affect the progression of Alzheimer's disease. Based on the results of his research, Dr. Strickland proposed a new model for the vascular component of Alzheimer's disease and in doing so has provided a promising gateway for the development of novel treatments.

What we who were in the Rockefeller University audience that evening, saw on Dr. Strickland's video presentation, was nothing less than astounding. As mentioned in the lecture, in the wild, mice are the natural prey of hawks, owls, and other flying predators, so they instinctively seek refuge when exposed on a flat surface. The experiment featured two groups of laboratory mice—one normal and one bred to develop Alzheimer's.

In the video, two of these mice—one from each group—were shown, one at a time, as they tried to find the escape hatch on a large round, flat table called a Barnes maze. The normal mouse found the escape hole within fifteen seconds. After almost a minute had elapsed, the Alzheimer's mouse was still searching.

Through new brain-imaging techniques, we were then shown what happened as the actual living Alzheimer's mouse was given an injection of a new compound developed to open up blood vessels in the brain that were clogged by amyloid-beta plaques. Right before our eyes we watched as these previously indissoluble plaques in the Alzheimer's mouse's brain disintegrated and normal blood flow was restored. The Alzheimer's mouse was then put back onto the Barnes maze, where it found the escape hole in less than thirty seconds. It is through such promising experiments as this one that dedicated medical researchers give us hope for an eventual cure for the disease that is ravaging so many people today, not the least of whom is our loved one.

Diabetes

Diabetes, another cause of vascular disease, is closely linked with a much higher risk of Alzheimer's disease. You can lower your blood pressure and control diabetes with diet, exercise, weight loss, and, if needed, medication. It is no secret that type 2 diabetes represents a very strong risk factor for dementia. Diabetes damages small blood vessels and may shrink parts of the brain. The cells in the brain run on ketones (a product of metabolized fat—in a process called ketosis) and glucose, a form of sugar which, according to the Mayo Clinic, is the brain's main source of fuel. But when the sugar is in the blood, it is not getting to the brain cells.

Blood sugar soars when the body makes insufficient insulin for glucose to enter the brain. Dr. Jae Hee Kang, assistant professor of medicine at Harvard Medical School and Boston's Brigham and Women's Hospital, has reported that insulin is the hormone that acts like a key to allow sugar into cells. In fact, according to Dr. Kang, some people call Alzheimer's disease type 3 diabetes. Moreover, insulin helps clear toxic beta-amyloid out of the brain. Dr. Angela Hanson, a physician at the University of Washington's School of Medicine, has reported that high insulin in the body means lower insulin in the brain. Cerebrospinal fluid also bathes the brain and the spinal cord to flush out these toxins.

Untreated, diabetes can cause many complications. Acute complications include diabetic ketoacidosis and coma. Serious long-term complications include cardiovascular disease, chronic renal failure, and diabetic retinopathy (retinal damage). Adequate treatment of diabetes is thus important, as is blood-pressure control and lifestyle factors such as stopping smoking and maintaining a healthy body weight.

The key to lowering sugar and insulin in the blood and raising it in the brain is to lose excess weight and exercise more. Dr. Hanson's experiments concluded that insulin may keep the brain healthy and that through diet, people with mild cognitive impairment can change their brain chemistry.

In 2012, a $7.9 million study was funded by the National Institutes of Health to test whether insulin administered via a nasal spray could help people with mild cognitive impairment or mild-to-moderate Alzheimer's. In the study, under the direction of Dr. Suzanne Craft, formerly of the University of Washington and now with Wake Forest University School of Medicine in North Carolina, current short-term pilot trials using intranasal insulin show higher cognitive function scores in people with mild cognitive impairment or early-stage Alzheimer's disease. Based on these results, longer-term trials will be run on pre-diabetics, as well as others at high risk for cognitive impairment.

Exercise

Studies have shown that exercise is not only beneficial for the body as a whole but it is also important for maintaining brain health. Exercising on a regular basis may increase a person's brain volume by causing small blood vessels to grow and expand their reach. Exercise also affects insulin production, blood flow, mood, and stress levels. Along with intellectual activity, consistent exercise for thirty to sixty minutes a day may serve to deter early symptoms of Alzheimer's disease. Along with a healthy diet, we need a healthy body workout. The earlier in life we start exercising, the sooner we can ward off the symptoms of multiple diseases, such as elevated blood pressure, obesity, diabetes, arthritis, and dementia. Exercising is also important to our immune system, which keeps us free from infection. Exercising also makes our bones strong, builds muscle, expands our breathing capacity, and raises our energy levels. We sleep better when we exercise, so our mood is better, and maybe even our sex life. Exercise also lowers anxiety.

Intellectual Activity

Many studies have shown that people, who have more education and have taken part in mentally stimulating activities throughout their lives have what is known as a cognitive reserve. Results of one study that tracked an older population over the course of eight years indicated that those who had a high cognitive reserve had a lower risk of Alzheimer's symptoms, regardless of their beta-amyloid levels. However, a cognitive reserve was protective in people with high levels of tau (tangles) a sign of more advanced disease. People who have better intellectual activity are somehow protected against the dementia of Alzheimer's. They may not be protected from the brain disease itself, but they're protected from the onset of symptoms.

Sleep

Adequate sleep is important for the whole body, including the brain. Why? All animals—fish; reptiles and amphibians; birds; and mammals, both marine and terrestrial—need sleep. But, as it turns out, many creatures, including dolphins, can survive only by sleeping in one hemisphere of the brain at a time, while the other hemisphere remains fully awake and on the lookout for predators. But our species has evolved to sleep in both hemispheres of the brain simultaneously.

But, how much sleep do we need?

For us humans, sleep is important. Getting enough sleep is necessary to give the body an opportunity to clear out the toxins and free radicals that have accumulated during the day and to prevent fatigue. The brain has only limited energy at its disposal, and it appears that it must choose between two different functional states—awake and aware or asleep and cleaning up. Cells in the brain, probably the glial cells which keep nerve cells alive, shrink during sleep. This increases the size of the interstitial space, the gaps between brain tissue, allowing more fluid to be pumped in and wash the toxins away.

Sleep is essential downtime to do some housekeeping to flush out neurotoxins.

But how does this relate to maintaining brain health and understanding

Alzheimer's disease? More research is required to see whether damage to the brain's waste-clearance system could lead to diseases like dementia. But it is important to note that many dementia-linked conditions, such as Alzheimer's or Parkinson's, are characterized by the build-up of damaged proteins in the brain. Problems with the brain's cleaning mechanism may contribute to such diseases. Even an hour more of sleep, a night, can do wonders for our physiological and neurological housekeeping chores. More sleep is better than less.

Diet

Alzheimer's specialists believe that following a Mediterranean diet can enhance brain function. The recommended diet is rich in plant-derived foods, fresh fruit, lean fish, and poultry, with moderate amounts of olive oil, low-fat yogurt, milk, and red wine and avoids refined carbohydrates, such as breads, pastas, soda, and sweets. Examples of specific recommended foods include

- Fish high in the omega-3 fatty acid DHA (wild salmon, albacore, herring, sardines)
- Berries (especially blueberries and strawberries)
- Seeds and nuts (flaxseeds, walnuts, pecans)
- Leafy green vegetables
- Cocoa powder
- Legumes (small red beans, pinto beans, black beans)
- Grape juice (no sugar added)
- Curry (or curry powder or turmeric)
- Whole grains
- Tea

Caffeine may protect your brain, if you consume four to five cups of coffee or tea per day. A good diet may enhance brain function.

There has also been an exploration of the positive effect of red wine on memory and cognition. Polyphenols is the plant compounds most closely associated with the protective effects of a daily glass of cabernet or pinot noir. It seems that the grape seed–derived polyphenolic extracts prevent the formation of beta-amyloid plaques, those aberrant neuron-destroying proteins found in the brains of people with Alzheimer's disease.

Now that we know what we should be doing, the goal is to make a commitment to start. Do what you can do and try to get to the goals outlined here: eat a better diet, exercise four to five times a week, and stay intellectually engaged and socially active. We all can start from where we are and try to get to goal. Good luck!

Stents—Hydrocephalus: Draining the Brain and the Family, Too

A number of people with Alzheimer's disease develop fluid on the brain. Bill developed this condition. Termed hydrocephalus, it prevents the brain fluid from going into the spinal cord and draining off excess fluid, which is what happens in a healthy person. Additionally, Bill had arthritis of the spine that was so severe the doctor could not get a needle into the spinal cord. The theory was that if the fluid on the brain could not be relieved, Bill would become incontinent and develop motor problems. Dr. Relkin, our neurologist, suggested that a neurosurgeon put a stent into the area of the brain where the fluid was accumulating, so as to empty it into the spinal cord.

After much thought, I agreed to this as a preventive measure and a way to maintain a certain amount of quality of life. However, it did not prove to be such. Before the surgery, Bill had walked to the hospital, talked, and showered, dressed, shaved, and fed himself. After the procedure, Bill was unable to function at the same level as before. He was incontinent and unable to walk, talk, or do anything for himself. Our neurosurgeon was reputed to be the best in the Northeast, but unfortunately, reputation and skill are not always matched.

This postsurgical situation presented a whole new set of circumstances.

Before the surgery, one person was able to attend to Bill and help him carry out the normal routine of the day. Now two people were needed to get him out of bed. He had to be fed, talked very little, and was not always coherent. Diapers became part of his attire. Suddenly, I was faced with the dilemma of trying to get two people to help around the clock at home or seeking an assisted-living facility. It was obvious that Bill would now need more care than before, such as physical therapy, occupational therapy, swallowing therapy, and speech therapy.

I was able to secure a medical placement in the neighborhood at the Kateri Residence, so our friends and his daughter, as well as I, could go every day to visit. My heart sank to watch the rapid deterioration in his condition. It was obvious that blood had bled into the brain. But rather than dwell on this new development, I had to see that immediate action was taken to help Bill regain some of his abilities and all available efforts were put forth to make his life as comfortable as possible.

Bill's daughter Mary Ellen began spending the entire day and evening with Bill, who was unable to talk to her. He spent the day silently in a wheelchair, at therapy, or in bed. This became a problem, as Mary Ellen become obsessed with her father's care. Soon, her siblings became concerned as well, and we all determined that Bill should be moved for a few months to a facility in South Carolina, where Bill's other daughter lived.

The Franke Home was wonderful, beautifully housed, and with a caring staff and all the medical-support teams Bill needed. Bill enjoyed being on an airplane for the flight from New York to South Carolina. He was smiling and very alert. Somehow, it must have reminded him of his many business trips. Yet, Bill's departure from New York on May 12, 2001, was fraught with emotion. Mary Ellen came to see Bill as he entered the car for the trip to the airport, but she refused to accompany us. I had handed her Bill's medical records to hold while we helped Bill into the car. When I held out my hand to get them back, she threw them on the sidewalk and walked away. The plan was for me to fly to Charleston on Thursday and stay until Monday.

Bill's daughter Catherine and his son-in-law lived near the Franke Home,

4. Understanding the Stages of Alzheimer's Disease

so Catherine was able to see Bill for part of each day. Catherine was doing a research project for the medical school in Charleston, so I thought she would be a good liaison for Bill and the Franke facility. This proved to be a nightmare! Catherine was very critical of the staff. If they did not respond immediately to her request, she became loud and angry.

On June 11, 2001, Catherine went to the administration at Franke to proclaim that she had the authority to determine all issues concerning Bill's care. She showed them a power of attorney that she had had an attorney draw up appointing herself Bill's guardian. Catherine knew this was not a valid power of attorney, but she tried to bluff her way into having Bill moved to another unit as she could not exert her will in the critical care unit. Her first request was to move Bill from the skilled-nursing unit, to the Alzheimer's unit, in spite of the fact that Bill needed skilled-nursing care, as he could not walk or feed himself and required physical therapy, occupational therapy, swallowing therapy, and general care due to incontinence, lack of bowel control, and bedsores.

The administrators asked that I tell Catherine that she must stop harassing the staff and accusing them of not responding to her requests in a timely manner. This was their second request and I was told that the next problem with Catherine would result in their discharging Bill. The next problem soon followed.

Catherine had read in a local paper that hospital aides usually had criminal records, so she began talking with other occupants' families about requiring Franke to do criminal background checks on all its employees. This caused a great deal of disruption among the staff, who naturally resented being thought of as criminals.

The Franke administration asked me to have Catherine desist or they would discharge Bill. I talked to Catherine about this decision and suggested that she should try to get along with the staff, as Bill was receiving excellent medical care. About the same time, Bill developed a bedsore, which happens when one is confined to a bed or wheelchair for an extended period of time. He was being treated for this, with satisfactory results.

One night, I received a call from the Franke Home stating that they had to see me immediately. Catherine had somehow hired an ambulance and abducted Bill late one night and taken him to the emergency room at the local hospital. They had refused to see him when they learned he was a resident of Franke. When Catherine tried to get Bill back into Franke, she was found out. The administration told me that Catherine would not be allowed on the site again, or they would transfer Bill to the county home. I told Catherine of this situation and stated that I would get a restraining order against her if she would not comply with the request. I insisted that she and her husband meet with the administration at once, so they would hear directly from the source what the outcome of this latest action was. Peace was achieved and Catherine and her husband agreed to cooperate with the staff at Franke.

While all this turmoil was going on, I was seeking guardianship of Bill, opposing the forces of his children, who were also trying to gain control of Bill's person, as well as his assets. The guardianship hearing, which was held in the Orphan's Court of Buck's County, was the only event that all three of Bill's children attended. Bill's children hired an attorney to represent them, and I had to as well, since it was assumed that our estate attorney would represent the best interest of Bill.

In order to determine if guardianship is appropriate, states have procedures that must be carried out, including an independent physician's examination and relevant witnesses. Once the criteria have been met, the court determines the outcome.

I filed a petition seeking guardianship, as did the attorney acting for the three children. The court ruled in my favor after the hearing, which included people from our bank and other relevant witnesses.

It was soon after this that Bill died, from the breakdown of his internal organs. Bill and I had promised Dr. Relkin that Bill would donate his brain and spinal cord for research, which was done. A memorial service was held for Bill some weeks later in New York, with a reception later for our friends. Only one of his children attended the service.

4. Understanding the Stages of Alzheimer's Disease

When You Suspect Something's Wrong: What You Should Do before Getting a Diagnosis

One day you notice something's not quite right. Previously, you may have thought, "Oh well, he is just becoming absent-minded or going through a temporary phase. As a person grows older, that is to be expected." Yet, now the scene has begun to change in a disturbing way. Perhaps there have been frequent memory lapses, signs of disorganization and disorientation, a decline in self-confidence, or you have noticed increased moodiness with episodes of high anxiety. You don't want to jump to conclusions, but you know that things seem to be getting worse, not better. You try not to panic, yet suddenly you realize that you must get some serious help. Where do you start?

First of all, you need to stop, breathe, and collect your thoughts. As Maria Shriver told the *Huffington Post* she felt when her father was diagnosed in 2003, you may feel confused, powerless, and alone.

Many times, we, as loving partners, concerned family members, or devoted friends, tend to ignore our own needs. It is normal to feel overwhelmed by the possibility that our loved one is suffering from a serious condition, but it is also important to maintain a sense of balance as we deal with the unknown. When it comes to a major change in health status on the part of our loved one, it is common for many people (especially spouses) to experience a sense of denial. Yet, as caring people, we must somehow find a way to overcome any perceived social stigmas related to a diagnosis of dementia and specifically to Alzheimer's disease. According to current medical protocol, there can, in fact, be no absolute diagnosis of this condition until autopsy. At that point, a definitive diagnosis of Alzheimer's disease can be made by linking clinical measures with an examination of brain tissue. However, doctors have several methods and tools to help determine, fairly accurately, whether a person who is having memory problems has possible Alzheimer's disease (symptoms may be due to another cause), probable Alzheimer's disease (no other cause for the symptoms can be found), or some other problem.

Once you have dealt with the initial shock that most of us experience when dealing with life-impacting health issues, it is important to map out a step-by-step strategy. Finding out what is causing the problem and determining how best to ensure proper treatment, communicating with friends and other family members, and setting up appropriate financial, legal, and caretaking arrangements.

Before you seek any kind of medical diagnosis or treatment (especially when dementia and Alzheimer's disease are possibilities), I want to emphasize, once again, that you should first take immediate steps to prevent perhaps irreversible financial problems. These steps are as follows:

1. Establish and/or update all legal documents and financial instruments, including trusts, wills, powers of attorney, guardianship assignment as well as ownership of securities, real property, and bank accounts;

2. Investigate health insurance coverage and Medicare, Medicaid, VA benefits or other entitlements, long-term health insurance policies, and Social Security and/or private disability eligibility.

3. Address healthcare treatment preferences, health proxies, and end-of-life directives.

4. Research private and/or government-subsidized (including military for veterans) options for in-home, out-patient, and institutional care.

5. Resolve any other financial arrangements that might impact the eligibility of your loved one to qualify for medical and long-term-care benefits such as Medicare and/or Medicaid.

In the best of all possible worlds, these issues will have been discussed and planned for long before the onset of any symptoms of cognitive impairment. If you find that these issues have not yet been addressed, please refer to other sections in this book, which describe important legal and financial options that are available to families, guardians, and caregivers of people with Alzheimer's and other dementias.

4. Understanding the Stages of Alzheimer's Disease

As you will see, the implications of a medical diagnosis are profound, because once the presence of any cognitive impairment—however mild—is confirmed, the legality of any changes to preexisting documents can be challenged. If you are—or think you may become—involved in a fiduciary capacity, do not hesitate to consult an attorney and/or financial advisor with expertise in the field of elder law before proceeding further with medical issues related to a possible diagnosis of dementia, including Alzheimer's disease.

Of course, it is vitally important to get a medical assessment, as soon as possible, so that further deterioration can be addressed and perhaps delayed, if not prevented. As you begin to review the conditions exhibited for past weeks and months, you should make a list of all the changes in behavior, habits, and attitudes that you have begun to notice. And remember, not all these symptoms necessarily mean the onset of Alzheimer's disease. In some instances, declining mental acuity and changing moods may be related to other conditions, such as low thyroid function, clinical depression, or even side effects from certain medications. So, as you begin to look for answers, it is important to know that there are many other forms of neurological impairment that are not due to Alzheimer's disease. Since not all dementias are the same, they can require different treatments. Before assuming that one is suffering from Alzheimer's disease, wait until his or her physicians have eliminated other possible conditions. For a more definitive diagnosis to determine the current extent of impairment, doctors will administer certain neuro-cognitive assessment tests (such as counting backwards from one hundred by sevens or filling in the blanks in a sentence). Other likely tests may include

- Looking for protein markers to see if certain amino acids related to the presence of brain disease are present
- Ascertaining any incidence of brain trauma or infection, such as bacterial meningitis
- Assessing the possibility of low thyroid function, clinical depression, pernicious anemia, vitamin deficiencies, and so on

- Examining certain genetic factors, such as a family history of dementia
- Eliminating other neurological conditions, including hydroencephalitus (hydrocephalus), or water on the brain; Huntington's, Parkinson's, and Pick's disease; as well as dementia with Lewy bodies and Creutzfeldt-Jakob disease (similar to mad cow disease).

At the first medical consultation, you should bring a list of all medications and corresponding dosages that your loved one takes, to enable the doctor to check for the possibility of adverse reactions and contraindications. Once all of those factors have been taken into consideration, you should let your physician know which symptoms have been experienced.

A hearing test should be administered, as hearing loss is often associated with and/or confused with dementia. Social isolation, which may come with hearing loss, is also a recognized risk factor for dementia. Those with hearing loss may sit through a dinner party and not hear a word. In America, studies I have read state that as many as 48 million people suffer some degree of hearing loss. If it can be clinically proven that hearing aids help delay or offset dementia, the benefits would be enormous, especially in terms of billions of dollars in health care savings.

There is also a strong correlation between the loss of the ability to smell and dementia. This is because the olfactory sensing centers in the brain lie near to the hippocampus areas, where memories are processed and stored. In Alzheimer's disease, memory loss is often associated with a demyelization (or gradual loss of the protective sheath around the neurons) of the hippocampi and subsequent shrinkage of these twin parts of the brain. A sniff test using peanut butter as the medium has been shown to be a good predictor of the likely presence of typical Alzheimer's-related neuronal destruction in the olfactory processing areas of the brain.

Sensory areas of the brain, such as the olfactory processing center and the hearing processing center, are often affected by neuronal degeneration before any other symptoms of Alzheimer's disease appear. Therefore, hearing and sniff tests can serve as essential screening parts of the testing profile.

Senior Moment or Alzheimer's Disease: How Can You Tell the Difference?

We've all been there at one time or another. You get up from your chair to go to the kitchen for a glass of milk and when you get to the kitchen, you forget what you came in for. What we have just experienced, in an otherwise rational existence, is that disconcerting interlude known as a senior moment—a brief lapse in memory or a moment of confusion. An example would be my going to my computer and forgetting whom I was going to email.

Such moments, while not particularly frequent, can nevertheless be unsettling, especially if we are also prone to misplace our keys, eyeglasses, or other often used accessories of daily living. However, if we carefully and immediately retrace our steps, we can usually remember why we got up out of our comfortable chair in the first place. And so, finally relieved at being back on track, we laugh at ourselves and mumble something about being overworked, easily distracted, or merely absentminded. Even if we haven't yet celebrated many midlife milestones, we may try to shrug off the incident by chalking it up to our advancing years.

When it comes to senior moments some new light has been shed on the subject, according to a recent article from a popular UK publication, the *Telegraph*, entitled "Brains of Elderly Slow Because They Know So Much." Based on a study published in the *Journal of Topics in Cognitive Science*, the article, by Sarah Knapton, states that scientists in the study believe that, much as a computer struggles as the hard drive gets full, older people do not decline mentally with age, it just takes them longer to recall facts because they have more information in their brains. This slowing down is not the same as cognitive decline. When comparing younger and older adult brains' processing time to computer speeds with smaller and larger-content databases, it is believed that the brains of older people do not get weak. On the contrary, they simply know more.

For those of us who are somewhat older, this is encouraging news indeed.

However, unlike the occasional senior moment we all will likely experience as we get on in years, Alzheimer's disease is, on the other hand, a devastating medical condition that will ultimately wreak havoc on every aspect of a person's existence, including their self-identity. Over time, it will impact their family, their future, and their finances, beyond the limits of just about any other disease on earth.

According to Dr. Tanzi in *Decoding Darkness*, "Alzheimer's is the most common type of dementia which unravels the tapestry of your life." In my opinion, this book is an authoritative source of information, based on scientific research and actual observation of people suffering from Alzheimer's disease. I recommend it strongly to anyone who wants an in-depth analysis of the way Alzheimer's affects the brain and of current efforts to discover how to treat this disease more effectively. Two of the contributors to this book, noted UCSD School of Medicine neuroscientist and physician George G. Glenner and his wife, Joy, felt such compassion for the sufferers and families impacted by Alzheimer's disease, that they set up Hillcrest, one of the first full-service adult-day-care facilities in California devoted exclusively to Alzheimer's and memory-loss patients and caregivers.

Author of more than 310 scientific publications, Dr. Tanzi is the Joseph P. and Rose F. Kennedy professor of neurology at Harvard University and director of the Genetics and Aging Research Unit at Massachusetts General Hospital. Also, the principal scientific founder of Prana Biotechnology, Ltd.; Genoplex, Inc.; and Neurogenetics, Inc., Dr. Tanzi lectures that Alzheimer's disease is a fatal brain disorder that not only annihilates a person's mind, but starts doing so years before it takes the person's life, which is surely its most insidious aspect. Its initial symptoms of forgetfulness and personality changes are ever so close to normalcy that they typically go unnoticed and once noticed, too long and unexplained. As the victim's grasp further slides, it can bring nothing but tormenting confusion for everyone.

Dr. Tanzi describes Alzheimer's, in short, as "the disease that robs the brain." While he concedes that exactly how this happens eludes us, he also admits that there is still plenty of confusion between the deficits of growing

4. Understanding the Stages of Alzheimer's Disease

older and those derived from a disease. This confusion is why it is often so difficult for family members to know if their loved one has begun to cross the line between having a few too many senior moments and exhibiting early symptoms of disease—whether these symptoms are caused by Alzheimer's or any other form of dementia.

Various tests, such as advanced imaging techniques, biochemical analysis, and mental function questionnaires, can indicate the presence of brain shrinkage, amyloid-beta plaques, tangles (tau), and increased numbers of glion cells (brain glue), all of which are indicative of Alzheimer's and differentiate Alzheimer's from other dementias, such as Huntington's disease, Pick's disease, and Creutzfeldt-Jakob and Lewy-body dementia among others. These tests can also help doctors in differentiating the typical symptoms of Alzheimer's from the presentation of other brain assaults such as head trauma and stroke.

By addressing these and other related medical issues in a timely fashion you and other family caregivers will be able to focus attention on other suddenly urgent priorities, such as

- Securing health insurance coverage, if not already in place
- Obtaining professional advice regarding legal and financial matters
- Accessing proper diagnostic testing and analysis and initiating treatment protocols
- Putting together a health care team, including medical providers, therapists and social workers, and caregiving support personnel
- Researching government initiatives, corporate family leave policies, and nonprofit programs that support Alzheimer's patients and their caregivers
- Setting up in-home and out-patient day-care arrangements
- Exploring long-term institutional care options

- Designating health proxies, care preferences, and end-of-life directives.

If you are a family member and/or a primary caregiver for one with Alzheimer's symptoms, you have no time to waste in setting up the protocols listed above, as well as initiating certain lifestyle changes and measures to prolong brain function, before the disease progresses to its next stage, the devastating loss of memory.

Is there anything we as individuals can do to stop this avalanche of brain disease? Unfortunately, completing all the crossword puzzles in the world and solving all the brain teasers online will not eliminate entirely the possibility that we, ourselves will someday become a victim of devastating dementia. Yet, despite this worrisome potentiality, it is possible for all of us—patients, families, and caregivers—to focus on preserving existing brain function and enhancing brain health.

So, even if one's specific genetic or medical profile puts one at higher risk for developing brain-related disorders, there are some helpful lifestyle habits we can put into practice to enhance brain health. While at this time, no one knows how to prevent Alzheimer's disease, what we can try to do is delay the onset of symptoms. According to many experts who promote healthy lifestyles as a means of maintaining brain function, simply following a daily exercise routine, lowering stress levels, getting enough sleep, staying mentally active, and adhering to a heart-friendly diet constitute some of the best ways to ward off both senior moments and dementia. I can virtually guarantee that your doctor will approve! Now that you have a program that will probably delay symptoms of early Alzheimer's disease, will you take the time to save your mind?

What Is Alzheimer's? Toward a Definition of the Disease

Alzheimer's disease is the most common form of dementia. There is no cure for the disease, which progressively worsens and eventually leads to death. It was first described by German psychiatrist and neuropathologist Alois Alzheimer in 1906 and was named after him.

4. Understanding the Stages of Alzheimer's Disease

Most often diagnosed in people over sixty-five, Alzheimer's disease develops differently for every individual. Cases of earlier onset also occur. Alzheimer's disease develops for an unknown and variable amount of time and can progress undiagnosed for years. The more intelligent the sufferer, the easier it is to mask the symptoms.

The first thing that comes to mind when we think of the causes of Alzheimer's disease is that it has a strong genetic component. You may think, "My grandmother had Alzheimer's and now my mom has it." It is with sadness that you make this connection when your own parent begins to exhibit symptoms of cognitive decline. Genetics play a major role in both types of Alzheimer's—the early-onset type, which appears before the age of sixty-five and the late-onset type, which manifests after the age of sixty-five. Other lines of investigation into possible causes of Alzheimer's involve not only the role of genetics in predisposing a person for the disease but also the role of genetic switches that allow this predisposition to express itself and manifest the symptoms of Alzheimer's. Current studies are now focusing on how genes are turned on and off, specifically what factors trigger a change in genetic expression, especially when it comes to Alzheimer's and other dementias, that has heretofore been dormant in an individual.

Some people who have inherited a genetic predisposition to developing Alzheimer's do not necessarily come down with the disease. If researchers can unlock the related genes and move them to the Off position, some people whose close kin have suffered from dementia might actually be spared from a devastating diagnosis.

While at this point, no one knows for certain what exactly causes this most common form of dementia, research indicates that in addition to genetic factors, Alzheimer's disease is associated with a high level of plaques and tangles in the brain. These plaques and tangles indicate the presence of Alzheimer's disease, but what causes or triggers the development of such aggregated proteins in the brain still remains, in large part, a mystery.

Public awareness must be raised to ensure a gentler approach to those who are compromised, through no fault of their own. We must also work to ensure greater community and governmental support for the caregivers (paid and unpaid alike) and other family members (such as long-distance caregivers) coping with their loved one's Alzheimer's.

According to the Alzheimer's Association Principles for a Dignified Diagnosis web report, it is important to include the patient in discussions of his or her situation. The main principles from this report that lead to more compassionate interactions between the one afflicted and all those involved medically and otherwise with his or her care are the following:

- Talk to me (the person with dementia) directly.
- Tell the truth.
- Test early.
- Take my concerns seriously, regardless of my age.
- Deliver the news in plain but sensitive language.
- Coordinate with other care providers.
- Explain the purpose of different tests and what you hope to learn.
- Give me tools for living with this disease.
- Work with me on a plan for healthy living.
- Recognize that am an individual; the way I experience this disease is unique.
- Alzheimer's is a journey, not a destination.

I would agree with these compassionate approaches and encourage caregivers to remember that although the loved one's memory and ability to function will fade as the disease progresses, there still abides a cherished person—an inviolate self—who needs to be recognized, respected, and responded to with all the love and patience we can give, despite the encroaching brain tangles and death of neurons that occur in Alzheimer's disease.

4. Understanding the Stages of Alzheimer's Disease

Diagnosing Alzheimer's Disease

To diagnose Alzheimer's disease, a primary doctor or a doctor trained in brain conditions (a neurologist) will review the medical history, medication history, and observed symptoms. The doctor will also conduct several tests. During the appointment, the doctor will evaluate

- Whether the patient has impaired memory or thinking (cognitive) skills
- Whether the patient exhibits changes in personality or behaviors
- The degree of the patient's memory or thinking impairment or changes
- How the patient's thinking problems affect the ability to function in daily life
- The cause of the patient's symptoms

Doctors may order additional laboratory tests or brain-imaging tests or may send the patient for memory testing. These tests can provide doctors with useful information for diagnosis, including ruling out other diseases that cause similar symptoms.

Doctors will perform a physical evaluation and check that the patient doesn't have other health conditions that could be causing or contributing to their symptoms, such as signs of past strokes, Parkinson's disease, or other medical conditions. The doctor may also order additional tests to rule out diseases that may be causing the observed symptoms, including laboratory tests to check for thyroid problems or vitamin B-12 deficiency and specific evaluations to determine if depression may be contributing to symptoms.

Assessing Memory Problems and Other Symptoms

To assess symptoms, the doctor may ask the patient to answer questions or perform tasks associated with their cognitive skills, such as their memory, abstract thinking, problem-solving, language usage, and related skills.

Mental-Status Testing
The doctor may conduct mental-status tests to test the patient's cognitive thinking and memory skills. Doctors use the scores on these tests to evaluate the degree of cognitive impairment.

Neuropsychological Tests
The patient may be evaluated by a specialist trained in brain conditions and mental-health conditions (a neuropsychologist). The evaluation can include extensive tests to evaluate the patient's memory and cognitive skills. These tests help doctors determine if the patient has dementia and if the patient can safely conduct daily tasks, such as driving and managing finances. Test results provide as much information on what the patient can still do as on what abilities may have been lost. These tests can also evaluate if depression may be causing the symptoms.

Interviews with Friends and Family
Doctors may ask family members or caregivers about the loved one's behavior. Doctors look for details that don't fit with the patient's former level of functioning. Family members or friends often can explain how the patient's cognitive skills, functional abilities, and behaviors have changed over time.

 This series of clinical assessments, the physical exam, and the setting (age and duration of progressive symptoms) often provide doctors with enough information to make a diagnosis of Alzheimer's disease. However, when the diagnosis isn't clear, doctors may need to order additional tests.

Laboratory Tests
Laboratory tests may be administered to rule out other disorders that cause some symptoms similar to those of Alzheimer's disease, such as a thyroid disorder or vitamin B-12 deficiency.

Brain-Imaging Tests
Alzheimer's disease results from the progressive loss, or degeneration, of brain cells. This degeneration may show up in a variety of ways in brain scans.

However, these scans alone aren't enough to make a diagnosis. Scans aren't used to diagnose the condition because there is overlap in what doctors consider normal age-related change in the brain and abnormal change. However, brain imaging can help

- Rule out other causes, such as hemorrhages, brain tumors or strokes
- Distinguish between different types of degenerative brain disease
- Establish a baseline about the degree of degeneration

The brain-imaging technologies most often used are computerized tomography, a CT scan, which uses X-rays to obtain cross-sectional images of the brain, and magnetic resonance imaging (MRI), which uses powerful radio waves and magnets to create a detailed view of the brain.

Future of Diagnosis

Researchers are working on new diagnostic tools that may enable doctors to diagnose Alzheimer's earlier in the course of the disease, when symptoms are very mild or before symptoms even appear.

Scientists are investigating disease markers and diagnostic tests, such as genes, disease-related proteins, and imaging procedures, which may accurately and reliably indicate whether a person has Alzheimer's disease and how much the disease has progressed. However, more research on these tests is necessary.

Benefit of an Early Diagnosis

Reluctance to go to the doctor when you or a family member has memory problems is understandable. Some people hide their symptoms, or family members cover for them. That's easy to understand because Alzheimer's is always about loss, such as loss of independence, loss of driving privileges, and loss of self. Many people may wonder if there's any point in a diagnosis, if there's no cure for the disease.

It's true that if a person has Alzheimer's or a related disease, doctors can't offer a cure. But getting an early diagnosis can be beneficial. Knowing what the person can do is just as important as knowing what he or she can't do. If a person has another treatable condition that's causing the cognitive impairment or somehow complicating the impairment, then doctors can start targeted treatments.

For those with Alzheimer's disease, doctors can offer drug and nondrug interventions that may ease the burden of the disease. Doctors often prescribe drugs that may slow the decline in memory and other cognitive skills. The patient may also be able to participate in clinical trials.

Additionally, doctors can teach the patient and their caregivers about strategies to enhance their living environment, establish routines, plan activities, and manage changes in skills to minimize the effect of the disease on their everyday life. Importantly, an early diagnosis also helps the patient, the family, and the caregivers plan for the future. Collectively, they will have the chance to make informed decisions about a number of issues, such as appropriate community services and resources, options for residential and at-home care, plans for handling financial issues, and expectations for future care and medical decisions.

When a doctor tells the patient and their family members about an Alzheimer's diagnosis, he or she will help them understand Alzheimer's, answer questions, and explain what to expect with Alzheimer's disease. Doctors will explain what capacities are preserved and how to limit future disabilities. They will look to discover untapped resources to keep the patient as healthy and safe as possible, with the least disruption in their daily activities.

Losing one's mind is perhaps the biggest fear all of us have at one time or another. Our minds are made of memories, piled up in layers over the years. What this really means is that we are afraid of losing our memory and along with it, our sense of self.

Many people are familiar with the lyrics to the award-winning song "Memory" from the musical *Cats*. In the poignant final moments of the musical, the aging cat-diva Grizabella relives her time of happiness and recaptures the memory of her "days in the sun." Sadly, for our loved ones who have Alzheimer's disease or other forms of dementia, most of their memories will be lost forever, and they may end up feeling alone and trapped in a strange and unfamiliar world.

In screening for dementia and determining the severity of cognitive impairment, including memory loss, doctors rely on in-depth medical and behavioral history as well as state-of- the-art neuroimaging. Memory and related cognitive function are also measured by standardized tests, such as the Mini-Mental State Examination (MMSE), or Folstein test; the Hodkinson Abbreviated Mental Test Score; and others. Implications of memory loss in Alzheimer's disease and other dementias-—as well as scientific, philosophical, and therapeutic ramifications about the nature of memory—are addressed. New directions in memory research are highlighted, with an emphasis on the impact this research can have on the ongoing search for a cure for Alzheimer's disease.

Memory Loss

People read about the memory loss caused by Alzheimer's disease and about age-related memory loss and try, often unsuccessfully, to understand the difference between these two disorders of memory loss—one progressive and devastating, the other comparatively benign. In the course of our lives, most of us will have to make important private and public decisions that involve a biological understanding of the mind. Some of these decisions will arise in the attempt to understand variations in normal human behavior, while others will concern more serious mental and neurological disorders.

When it comes to deciding whether one is merely becoming more forgetful or may be starting to develop significant memory loss, we need to ask how memory loss due to Alzheimer's disease can manifest. According to the Alzheimer's Association, short-term memory loss is indicative of the possible onset of mild cognitive impairment and/or Alzheimer's. Why is this loss of recently learned information significant when the person seems to remember the remote past so clearly? To understand this phenomenon, we need to first ask how memories are formed in the first place.

Memory does not exist in a single site or region of the central nervous system. There are estimated to be 10 to 100 billion neurons in the human brain, each neuron making about one thousand connections to other neurons at the junctions called synapses. Learning and then storing what we learn through life involve intricate changes in the nature and number of trillions of neuronal connections.

Neuroimaging

New tests have been developed in in vivo imaging probes targeted to amyloid-beta protein. Additional advances included automated volumetric imaging methods to quantitate cerebral loss. Structural, molecular, and functional imaging techniques can give us a window on the etiology of Alzheimer's disease and other neurodegenerative diseases.

Cognitive Testing for Memory Loss

Several standardized testing formats exist to evaluate early signs of cognitive, memory, or thinking impairments to help physicians know how well one's brain is working.

The MMSE is the most commonly used cognitive evaluation for memory loss. As a screening test, it doesn't delve deeply into someone's mental functioning across different areas of intellectual performance. The MMSE is a brief, thirty-point questionnaire that samples functions including arithmetic, memory, and orientation. Other brief tests are also used, such as the Hodkinson Abbreviated Mental Test Score, or the General Practitioner Assessment of Cognition.

Longer formal tests are used for deeper analysis of specific deficits. The Self-Administered Gerocognitive Exam is designed to detect early signs of cognitive, memory, or thinking impairments. It evaluates your thinking abilities and helps physicians to know how well your brain is working. It is an informational service to be self-administered by the patient but scored by his or her physician. It is not intended to diagnose any specific condition but can help doctors determine if further evaluation is necessary.

In addition to the standardized testing formats mentioned above, a new

4. Understanding the Stages of Alzheimer's Disease

cognitive function test has been designed to differentiate between the mild cognitive impairment of Alzheimer's disease and that of normal aging. Being able to connect a person's name with his or her face is one example of relational memory. These two pieces of information are stored in different parts of the brain, but the hippocampus binds them so that the next time you see that person, you remember his or her name.

Our senses of smell and taste also bear a unique burden of memory. This is because smell and taste are the only senses that connect directly to the hippocampus, the center of the brain's long-term memory.

To keep a memory, you need to keep having the memory, revisiting the memory, using it, so as to keep that collection of neurons imprinted and those synaptic connections in place. If they're not used, then they wither.

To remember things, you need to go through the process of remembering them again. You make a new memory each time you remember, revisiting the route from neuron to neuron. Researchers have discovered that there is an actual anatomical change in the laying down of long-term memories. The axons grow new synapses and new proteins are made in the nucleus of the neuron. There's a change at the cellular level, something that doesn't occur in the making of short-term memories.

In order to convert a short-term memory into a long-term one, I have learned that we need to care about it enough to do so, whether for happy or unhappy reasons and that our caring has physiological effects. It seems that via quantity or quality—either via repetition, thinking about something over and over, or by means of the intensity of a shock—equivalent emotional events create the memory. When you remember, it's a memory of the memory that you're having.

There are four levels of memory. The first is Sensory Memory, which is all the stuff our eyes see.

The second level is the Working Memory, which is the material we hold in mind, temporarily, until we need it. Then we forget it.

Short-term memory is defined as things we did today, yesterday, and last weekend. The process of converting a select few of these into long-term memories, forming strong memories that survive, can take weeks, and scientists think most of the work is done while we sleep.

Branches of Long-Term Memory

- Implicit memory is another way of defining procedural memory, the one that deals with the things that we do as if automatically. Riding a bike, driving a car, knowing a dance, playing the flute—these skill memories are taken care of by the cerebellum in league with the basal ganglia, four clusters of neurons at the base of the brain that help initiate and control movement. Serotonin is the neurotransmitter of choice in the making of implicit memories, and dopamine in the creating of explicit memory.
- Explicit memory is the sort we need to call up actively; "thinking" in the familiar conscious sense.
- Episodic memory is autobiographical and locates things in time and sequence.
- Semantic memory is encyclopedic and intellectual, for facts.

Alzheimer's disease damages the episodic, or autobiographical, memory first and worst. The semantic survives longer. Sufferers might know very little about themselves and nothing whatsoever about what happened ten minutes ago and yet might be able to talk at length about the battles and the princes associated with the history of a ruined castle.

What we see, the way that we see it, and the way we remember it are essentially subjective. The process of making memories and then remembering them, is both technical and personal. Our memories of things are never objective. We interact with them and add meaning to them.

To better understand the nature of memory and, by extension, to more fully understand how Alzheimer's disease impacts memory in addition to memory's classification into the two most familiar categories, long-term and short-term, we must also look at what constitutes implicit memory and what constitutes explicit memory. This distinction is important because where these different types of memories are stored is impacted by the progression of Alzheimer's disease. First, memory is a distinct mental function, clearly separate from other perceptual, motor, and cognitive abilities. Second, short-term memory and long-term memory can be stored separately. Third, at least one type of memory can be traced to specific places in the brain.

Implicit Memory

Implicit memory is not a single memory system but a collection of processes involving different brain systems that lie deep with the cerebral cortex. Implicit memory often has an automatic quality. It is recalled directly through performance, without any conscious effort or even awareness that we are drawing on memory. Those experiences are virtually inaccessible to conscious recollection.

The second principle mentioned above holds the key to memory loss in Alzheimer's disease, as the hippocampus is the brain area first impacted by Alzheimer's plaques and tangles, which cause neuronal death. Loss of medial temporal lobe structures, particularly loss of the hippocampus, destroys the ability to convert new short-term memory to new long-term memory.

Explicit Memory

Explicit and implicit memories are processed and stored in different regions in the brain. In the short term, explicit memory for people, objects, places, facts, and events is stored in the prefrontal cortex. These memories are converted to long-term memories in the hippocampus and then stored in the parts of the cortex that correspond to the senses involved—that is, in the same areas that originally processed the information.

Clinical Trials: Experimental Protocols in Search of New Therapies

You may become aware of clinical trials being conducted and consider participating. Bill and I did so upon the recommendation of our doctors. These experimental protocols are searching continually for new therapies and are vital for informing research and treatment.

Clinical trials are defined by MedicineNet as "Trials to evaluate the effectiveness and safety of medications or medical devices, by monitoring their effects on large groups of people." The site continues with descriptions of who conduct such trials, how recruitment is handled, how the trials are constructed using a control group and a placebo, what experimental and follow-up protocols are used, and how government agencies use results from clinical trials to approve or disapprove experimental treatments for promising new drugs. Clinical-research trials may be conducted by government health agencies such as the National Institutes for Health (NIH), researchers affiliated with a hospital or university medical program, independent researchers, or private industry.

Usually volunteers are recruited, although in some cases research subjects may be paid. Subjects are generally divided into two or more groups, including a control group that does not receive the experimental treatment, receives a placebo (inactive substance) instead, or receives a tried-and-true therapy for comparison purposes. Typically, government agencies approve or disapprove new treatments based on clinical-trial results. While important and highly effective in preventing obviously harmful treatments from coming to market, clinical-research trials are not always perfect in discovering all side effects, particularly effects associated with long-term use, and interactions between experimental drugs and other medications.

For some patients, clinical-research trials represent an avenue for receiving promising new therapies that would not otherwise be available. Patients with difficult to treat or currently "incurable" diseases may want to pursue participation in clinical-research trials if standard therapies are not effective. Clinical-research trials are sometimes lifesaving.

According to the Alzheimer's Association, recruiting and retaining clinical-trial participants is now the greatest obstacle, other than funding, to developing the next generation of Alzheimer's treatments. Without participation, finding a cure is virtually impossible.

4. Understanding the Stages of Alzheimer's Disease

Clinical trials are also important in furthering Alzheimer's research and treatment because they can potentially

- Establish a deeper understanding of how Alzheimer's disease is caused or triggered
- Uncover ways to effect earlier detection of the disease
- Enable doctors to initiate treatment before a person at high risk becomes symptomatic or cognitively impaired

At this point you may be thinking: If someone with Alzheimer's wants to participate in a clinical trial, what is the best way to go about it? The Alzheimer's Association website has a TrialMatch section, which can be accessed through the following link: www.alz.org/trialmatch.

5

Legal and Financial Matters

The Importance of Being Well-Informed and Well Organized

This part of my book has been prepared by Julia Cheung, a lawyer and friend whose grandfather suffers from Alzheimer's disease. Many people who are responsible for someone with Alzheimer's disease may not even realize that legal and financial matters are of the utmost importance when a diagnosis of probable Alzheimer's is looming. Here are some of the ways you can prepare for dementia caregiving, get better organized with paperwork, and lessen some of the inevitable personal, legal, and financial challenges:

- Place the requisite legal documents and healthcare directives in a file while your relative or friend is still capable of making decisions. This is one way of ensuring a less stressful journey into caregiving.

- Learn how to deal with other time-sensitive issues, such as obtaining primary and supplementary health and long-term-care insurance coverage. Applying for disability insurance or other health-related entitlements from the military, other governmental agencies, or employers is one way of protecting yourself and your loved ones from the extraordinary drain

5. Legal and Financial Matters

that Alzheimer's disease can be to family finances.

- Investigate Alzheimer's support groups and other community or faith-based organizations. In many communities across the country, not-for-profit groups such as these offer ongoing support for adult-day-care options, hands-on help with activities of daily living, caregiver respite, and assistance with meal delivery or preparation, as well as group settings where you can maintain exercise routines for your loved one. These groups can also be a valuable resource for local volunteers to help with transportation needs, food shopping, recreational activities, and companion services. By taking full-advantage of the low-cost (or even free) services provided by local nonprofit organizations, you may be able to avoid extra expenses and delegate some of the tasks involved in Alzheimer's caregiving.

As you come face-to-face with all the challenges that Alzheimer's poses, it is imperative to remember that you don't have to face them alone. Only a decade or so ago, this was not necessarily the case. Many people were isolated as they struggled to structure their finances, obtain proper care for their loved ones, and access information about the disease. However, as Alzheimer's awareness continues to grow in this country and abroad, governmental and private funding for research is increasing and dementia support groups and websites are springing up. With the advent of twenty-four-hour Alzheimer's hotlines, dementia-specific care units, elder care specialists, and caregiver blogs, there are many more resources than ever before—both online and in person—now available to help you.

Not only is Alzheimer's awareness increasing day by day but people are beginning to fight for much-needed changes in our society regarding pressing issues of this devastating disease by lobbying against the stigma that dementia in one's family once involved and advocating on behalf of more funding for research and patient/caregiver support.

Celebrities are writing memoirs and making films about their experiences and encounters with Alzheimer's. Scientists, physicians, and members of Congress are spreading the word that Alzheimer's is no longer a shameful issue to be ignored. International medical conferences are being convened to underscore the reality that Alzheimer's disease is now on the verge of becoming a worldwide epidemic that must be eradicated.

Being a caregiver to a loved one with Alzheimer's disease can be overwhelming. You may be a spouse who is now suddenly responsible for household finances or a business unfamiliar to you. You may be a son or a daughter who must now know the details of a medical record for a mom or a dad whom you have always seen as invincible. Whoever you are, accepting the role of caregiver shows tremendous courage. Taking care of an Alzheimer's patient is an onerous task that demands a great amount of time, patience, and energy; however, it is also an opportunity for self-discovery. By helping the patient cope with his or her deteriorating abilities, as a caregiver, you will also learn to trust your conscience and understand what it means to love unconditionally. The road ahead will be challenging, but as you will see, there is much in your power to help the Alzheimer's patient and you continue to live joyful and meaningful years.

Getting the conversation started with family members and love ones about health care, financial, and estate planning is the first step. Family and friends of an individual with Alzheimer's disease, stressed by the impending loss of a loved one, frequently feel uncomfortable—even about discussing matters of money and mortality. Good planning and prior discussion can relieve anxiety for everyone about carrying out the patient's wishes. Thus, as caregiver, you should encourage the patient to start making important decisions early on, and if needed, take charge of the process. Help them understand that delay or avoidance can prove costly and cause unnecessary conflicts, anger, time loss, and confusion later. If you are currently caring for a patient who no longer has the mental capacity to make decisions, you may have to secure guardianship to make plans on his or her behalf (refer to the section on guardianships). Know that pragmatism and sensitivity can go hand in hand.

It is important to have dialogues with loved ones, doctors, attorneys, and other professionals. Review all options for the patient and understand what legal tools will best suit his or her needs. It is important for the patient to designate individuals for specific roles as soon as possible, such as the person to be the executor for the will or the guardian for the children. Use the checklists provided to start organizing personal assets and begin coordinating with an attorney to draft the necessary documents.

You are not alone. As research efforts and public awareness of Alzheimer's disease continue to grow, resources and communities for caregivers have also expanded remarkably. One recent study of Alzheimer's caregivers found that 75 percent had unmet needs and did not know where to access outside services like transportation, home-delivered meals, respite, and support groups (see Family Caregiver Alliance at caregiver.org). Remember, even though there may be many aspects of Alzheimer's disease beyond anyone's control, you and your loved ones will always have the power to plan a secure future.

Money, Aging, and Alzheimer's:

Longevity Planning, Long-Term-Care Insurance, Medicare, Medicaid, and Supplemental Insurance

Because most people with late-stage Alzheimer's end up needing costly, full-time, and/or long-term nursing care, it is necessary at the onset for families and caregivers to address these critically important matters: longevity planning, long-term-care insurance, Medicare- and Medicaid-eligibility requirements, and coverage issues, as well as other entitlements, such as veteran's benefits, Social Security disability, and supplemental health insurance.

Until suddenly faced with an enormous bill, many people do not realize that long-term nursing home care is not paid for by Medicare, which covers only short-term stays in a skilled-nursing facility following hospitalization for seniors and disabled people who qualify for Medicare. At this writing, Medicare pays for only a limited number of days of rehabilitation in a nursing home and after that, you are on your own. In the United States, a nursing home resident (spouse or guardian in some instances) can become personally responsible (liable) for upward of $500 a day for long-term, custodial care unless or until he or she has long-term-care insurance or qualifies for Medicaid and/or veteran's benefits.

Additionally, many people in the United States also do not realize that Alzheimer's disease can cost more than $200,000 per patient. This is well beyond the means of the average family in America. In fact, according to the Shriver Report, only 7 percent of people in the United States have long-term-care insurance. As the result, may family caregivers have no option but to care for their loved one at home—often at great personal sacrifice and without compensation. In fact, according to the Alzheimer's Association Facts and Figures for 2018, in 2013, 16 million caregivers provided an estimated 17.7 billion hours of unpaid care valued at more than $220 billion. No doubt, many of these hours were required to care for dementia sufferers in the United States who were not covered by long-term-care insurance. Julia's aunt gave up her job to care for her father.

Due to the limited scope of this book, it is not possible to go into great detail about specifics relating to obtaining long-term-care and other supplementary health-insurance coverage. However, as a brief introduction, you will find information from what I believe is one of the most helpful and comprehensive sources I have found on the subject: *What Your Doctor Won't Tell You About Getting Older: An Insider's Survival Manual for Outsmarting the Health-Care System* by Mark Lachs, MD, MPH, director of Geriatrics at New York Presbyterian Health System, and professor of medicine at Weill Cornell Medical College.

No one likes to think of life-and-death issues in such an impersonal way, especially when these issues concern oneself or someone much beloved. But like it or not, this is a matter every responsible caregiver must take seriously and address in a timely manner. Dr. Lachs offers families some very practical steps to approaching an often painful and difficult subject: how long a particular individual (that is, their loved one) can reasonably expect to live. His words and advice follow below. For my readers' convenience, I have also included some corresponding websites on longevity planning that Dr. Lachs cites.

5. Legal and Financial Matters

- Start with actuarial life expectancy as a guide, but don't fully rely on it.
- A good place to start is with Social Security's actuarial table:
- www.socialsecurity.gov/OACT/STATS/table4c6.html
- Refine the estimate by factoring in your health habits and medical history.

  Consider making adjustments for smoking history, hypertension, or other common medical problems. Visit websites that calculate your physiological age, as opposed to chronological age, based upon a variety of variables that are known to be predictive, such as:

  www.realage.com (created by Dr. Michael Roizen and Dr. Mehmet Oz) and

  www.livingto100.com (created by Dr. Tom Perls)

- Factor in specific medical problems.

  These include illnesses such as: rheumatoid arthritis, emphysema, and Parkinson's Disease.

- Make predictions about your functional abilities as you age.

  Strong family histories of diseases that increasingly appear to be at least partially inheritable (such as Alzheimer's Disease) should be considered in this process. Remember the old adage: "Man makes plans and God laughs." Imprecision is not a valid excuse for avoiding the topic entirely; you've got to make some reasonable guestimate of longevity, if you plan to do it appropriately.

- The time to start understanding Medicare and Medicaid is now.

Understanding how the programs reimburse for various expenses, such as rehabilitation or a nursing home stay, can influence your decision to buy long-term care insurance . . . and it can help you help a parent wade through the issues they are facing. My favorite unbiased Web source for information on the programs is the Kaiser Family Foundation's site: www.kff.org/medicaid and www.kff.org/medicare

- Long-term care insurance: not "if" but "when."

It usually goes into effect when you develop two or more impairments in Activities of Daily Living (ADL)—tasks like bathing and eating. And just like any other health-related coverage, long-term care insurance gets more and more expensive as you get older, especially if you develop chronic diseases that are likely to worsen and be associated with disability in their later course. The horror stories range from insurance companies that have simply gone bankrupt after you've paid into a policy for years, to ridiculous fine-print clauses like exclusions for dementia—the reason more than 50 percent of people ultimately come to need long-term care insurance. Then there are the companies that simply won't pay when the policy is supposed to go into effect.

Other things you may not know about long-term care insurance that should increase its appeal: many states offer tax benefits to purchasers. Federal employees have access to an unusually good program. And some states have partnership programs with private insurance companies (such as the

5. Legal and Financial Matters

opportunity to legally shelter your assets from Medicaid for a spouse, so you get care and s/he keeps the fruits of your retirement savings. A favorite resource for researching long-term care insurance is the National Clearinghouse for Long-Term Care Information. This site includes an excellent, unbiased discussion on the topic: www.longtermcare.gov/LTC/Main Site/Paying LTC/Private Programs/LTC lnsurance/index.aspx

- Consider supplemental health insurance.

Medicare doesn't pay for a ton of stuff and the list of uncovered needs is only going to get longer. For example, it won't pay for medical care anywhere outside the United States. Nor does it pay for the first three units of blood you need in an accident or emergency. "Medigap" insurance pays for many of the things Medicare won't, but no longer covers prescription drugs. Gap policies for drugs, known as Medicare supplemental prescription plans can be purchased separately. The best time to buy a Medigap policy is in the open-enrollment period (the first six months after you turn sixty-five and become eligible for Medicare, because you can't be refused coverage; don't have a waiting period before coverage starts and can't have your premiums increased because of new or worsening health problems.

The best information on Medigap policies come from the Federal government's site: ww.medicare.gov/medigap/Default.asp Be sure to download the associated guide "Choosing a Medigap Policy" which is indispensable and superb (and perhaps the only effective tool in trying to understand this complicated topic: www.medicare.gov/Publications/Pubs/pdf/02110.pdf

Other helpful tips for caregivers who are in charge of organizing the affairs of their loved one and delegating tasks to family members are listed below:

- Get everybody on the same page
- Small steps, first ... they add-up
- If help is required at home, you'll need to do some matchmaking.

The following information has been complied specifically for this book by a professional who deals with legal and financial matters. I want to remind readers that there are many other important considerations that come into play when you are trying to provide proper care for someone without bankrupting the entire family. Consultation with a geriatric social worker or specialist in Elder Care and/or an attorney with expertise in this practice area can be well worth the expense. Some people might also want to consult a certified financial planner or trust and estates attorney, especially if there are significant assets involved. Nevertheless, whether a person diagnosed with Alzheimer's Disease is wealthy or not, there are a few important issues that should be addressed at length in these consultations to determine which ones apply to your own situation. These include:

- Government Programs
    - Medicare, Medicaid—Income, Asset, and Time Requirements
    - Changes to be implemented as a result of the Affordable Care Act (Obamacare)

- Costs of Various Care Options: Available, but usually very expensive
    - At Home- Family members, friends, paid help
    - Non-caregivers to handle non-health related tasks: financial assistants, bookkeepers, case workers, etc.
    - Adult day care
    - Nursing Homes and Assisted Living Residences
    - Special Alzheimer's Disease Units
    - Caregiver Respite Options

There are also work-related issues that could apply to either the person with cognitive impairment or the primary caregiver, or both, such as family leave options under The Family and Medical Leave Act of 1993 (FMLA):

The Family and Medical Leave Act of 1993 (FMLA) is a United States Federal Law requiring covered employers to provide employees job-protected and unpaid leave for qualified medical and family reasons. Qualified medical and family reasons include personal or family illness, family military leave, pregnancy, adoption, or foster care placement of a child. The FMLA is administered by the Wage and Hour Division of the United States Department of Labor and available on their website.

This government program, FMLA, was intended "to balance the demands of the workplace with the needs of families." The Act allows eligible employees to take up to 12 work weeks of unpaid leave during any 12-month period to attend to the serious health condition of the employee, parent, spouse or child, or for pregnancy or care of a newborn child, or for adoption or foster care of a child. In order to be eligible for FMLA leave, an employee must have been at the business at least 12 months and worked at least 1,250 hours over the past 12 months and work at a location where the company employs 50 or more employees within 75 miles. The FMLA covers both public and private sector employees, but certain categories of employees are excluded, including elected officials and their personal staff members.

Should you or any others on your caregiving team be interested in researching in more detail what FMLA has to offer, especially in terms of the revised definitions of "adult child," "spouse" and "elderly parent" you may find the following websites helpful:

http://www.dol.gov/whd/fmla/ and/or

http://www.nationalpertnership.org/research-library/work-family/fmla/guide-to fmla.pdf

Other work-related issues that should be addressed when an employed caregiver finds it necessary to devote more time to Alzheimer's caregiving responsibilities include:

- Flexible work hours and/or job-sharing possibilities; Options for early retirement;
- Pension eligibility and the financial impact of taking time-off for caregiving; Extended medical, disability and life insurance coverage for the caregiver; and Social Security benefits and/or employee-based disability coverage.

As families try to comprehend the financial ramifications of Alzheimer's and cope with the lifestyle changes required to ensure the safety and care of their loved one with impending or active dementia, sooner or later one common, but serious, problem will come to the surface. And this one problem, if not addressed, can determine the best laid plans and intentions in the world: "no caregiver burn-out."

The fact is, that in all too many cases, the needs of the primary caregiver are often overlooked. The basic needs of many over-burdened caregivers who—in the face of severe sleep deprivation, inadequate emotional support and/or dwindling financial resources, are often forced to make unprecedented personal sacrifices—are rarely given sufficient attention, if not entirely ignored.

Therefore, when you meet with experts and family members to evaluate options and plan strategies, it is essential that in all of these discussions the well-being and financial situation of the caregiver be given as much attention as the health issues and care options of the person who has Alzheimer's. Too often, many harried and stressed-out caregivers become depressed and ignore their personal health and well-being, even to their own detriment. And, if the primary caregiver loses his or her mental or physical health, it is ultimately to the detriment of the patient. Therefore, when dealing with the impact of Alzheimer's caregiving on the primary care provider, all family members, all supplementary caregivers and supportive friends, as well as the professional medical team—whether or not they are personally involved in hands-on caregiving—should become aware that caregiver burn-out must be avoided at all cost. Indeed, caregiver burn-out is a serious matter of life and death and will be addressed at greater length.

For the moment, however, let us be reminded that whatever practical support systems—whether emotional, financial, legal or health-related, can be successfully put into place at the outset, or preferably even before Alzheimer's is officially declared, will pay off in reducing the stress level of everyone involved in dementia caregiving. In the meantime, let us now turn our attention to the practical matter of ensuring safety for our Alzheimer's-impaired loved ones, both at home and in transit.

Wills and Other Legal Documents: Where There Is a Will, There Must Be a Way—A Way Out

Control of Bill's money seemed to present personal challenges for many people. My absence on business trips to the Far East afforded the perfect opportunity for Bill's children to pressure their father to change his will. Catherine, who lived in South Carolina, was the main instigator in this effort and, as soon as I departed for my trip, would move into our guest room. Bill was very agitated during these visits by his daughter, who was joined in this effort by his other daughter, Mary Ellen, who lived in New York. When I spoke with Bill, he would express his anxiety and ask why they were interfering with his affairs.

In 1990 Bill had set up a separate stock account in my name, as he told me his children would be a problem for me at his death. At our wedding in 1979, Catherine and her brother did not attend. His youngest daughter, Mary Ellen, who lived with us, did attend. I thought it odd but did not question it.

For our entire married life, Bill and I had managed our investments with the advice of our bank. Meetings were arranged with the bank staff in attendance as well as our legal and estate attorney, Brian Price. The bank attorneys and our attorney suggested dividing Bill's wealth into two trusts so that his children's share would be segregated from my share. A very useful suggestion.

This was done to protect me from possible law suits from Bill's children after his death. As his children were childless, trusts were executed as charitable trusts for tax reasons and paid out over a period of time and eventually to certain charities. This was not well received by his children, so they instigated a series of wills that were drawn up over a period of time, leaving the bulk of the estate to the children and various individuals that they thought could be helpful to them.

It is important to research legal requirements of the state you reside in as many states, including Pennsylvania, have legal requirements concerning inheritance. Pennsylvania requires that a husband leave his wife one third of his estate. Local Bucks County lawyers were asked by Bill's children to draw up new wills and did so, often naming themselves as executor at very generous fees. Bill would sign these as they were done when I was working outside the country. I asked Bill why he would sign them, and he said his children exerted so much pressure it was easy to give in and then give me a copy of the new will.

Guardianship

This untenable situation necessitated that I seek guardianship of Bill so he would not have to endure this kind of harassment and also to protect me. I had to hire independent counsel to act for me as it would be a conflict of interest for Bill's estate attorney to represent me in such matters.

Since Bill's daughter Mary Ellen worked for Gear, she became aware that I was seeking guardianship. This prompted Catherine to immediately seek an attorney in Bucks County to draw up a new will enriching the siblings and bribing the housekeeper in Bucks County with financial rewards to remain silent about her bringing an attorney to our Pennsylvania home there.

Guardianship procedures are regulated by the states and have certain criteria that must be met. As soon as Bill's children learned I was seeking to be named Bill's guardian, they started a lawsuit to name the three of them as guardian. This required a court hearing with Bill's children's lawyer presenting their argument and my attorney presenting my case. The court ruled in my favor.

All this was happening when Bill was obviously declining. As the result, it took a lot of time and effort for Bill to express his wishes. Guardianship is a very important matter to protect the integrity and wishes of the person with Alzheimer's disease. You should be prepared to know how to protect these wishes. It requires research and perhaps hiring legal counsel.

Family Matters—Stress and Elder Abuse: Possible Precipitating Factors of Dementia Onset

Elizabeth Loewy, the Manhattan assistant district attorney for elder abuse at that time, told me that people suffering from Alzheimer's and other diseases affecting the aging are vulnerable to many groups of people: family members, professional advisors, acquaintances, and con artists. One often finds out about these incidents by reading newspapers or talking to the relatives and friends of the victims.

Our friend and gardener, Pamela Berdan, was the victim of a con artist who knew of her attachment to her cat, in her later years. He promised that for a fee of $5,000, he could have the cat featured on the cover of a major magazine. Only when she asked me to purchase the magazine for her, did I learn of this scam and was able to report him to the police.

For two savvy people like Bill and me, it was hard to believe that we ourselves could fall victim to children, housekeepers, educators, and professionals. Preparing for aging, before one becomes old, seems the only way and I have included within this book a list of things one needs to be aware of and monitor. The challenge is when to initiate the steps, such as taking away the right to sign checks, trade in securities, limiting amounts on credit cards, and needing to disallow signing documents regarding financial transactions. Timing is everything and always a thorny matter as you are taking away one of the means by which a person defines him or herself.

Dealing with close family members adds an additional burden to this problem. I had been warned by Bill that I would have trouble with his children, but as life was going along without major problems, I did not dwell on that likelihood.

While the legal problems generated by Bill's children were occurring, I adjusted to the new Bill. He enjoyed having friends visit and could still talk about subjects he had been interested in earlier in his life. Our friends were understanding and never made him feel awkward or out of touch. We limited company at dinner parties to people who were long-time friends.

We continued to have close friends dine with us, through Christmas of 2000, when we entertained twenty-four guests—all friends and family. Bill loved the Christmas decorations and presents.

Elder Abuse: Scam Artists Are Everywhere

Since 1983, my firm, Gear, had contract agreements with a major Japanese retail group, Isetan, for two decades in order to implement our coordinated home-fashions program for the Japanese market. As many products were manufactured in China, this meant a ten- to fifteen-day trip to Japan and China twice a year for me and Gear staff.

When I had to go for two weeks to China to work I entrusted the daily care of Bill to Mary O'Rahilly, whom we knew from church and who had been working as a companion for Bill for some time; as well as a cook and a butler, both as live-in help, so Bill was never left alone. Mary informed me that an acquaintance of ours had been showing up at the noon mass, which Bill often attended, and was taking Bill to lunch afterward. Since Mary was not included in the lunch invitation, she waited for him in the foyer of the restaurant. Bill was not supposed to have alcohol with his medications and Mary was alarmed that Bill was drinking at lunch. At the same time, our priest called me and asked to speak with me about Bill. It seemed he had observed the interest that a certain parishioner was taking in Bill. Father Boniface knew of Bill's illness and thought that Ruth Reardon, the parishioner, was coming on too strong in pursuing Bill at mass.

At the same time, I discovered that checks totaling $100,000 had been deposited to Ruth Reardon's investment company. Ruth Reardon was a former faculty member at Marymount Manhattan College. (We had met her, casually, at the college.) When I asked Bill about the checks to her company, he explained that the funds were to build a nuclear power plant in Bangladesh and then showed me a card of the consul general of Bangladesh. Bill's former company had been involved in building such plants in Japan, so Bill was excited that he was being included as an advisor, as well as, an investor.

I had our corporate attorney send Ruth Reardon a letter stating that Bill was suffering from Alzheimer's and requesting that his investment into her fund be accounted for and returned. Bill was furious that the word "Alzheimer's" was used. I then went through the mail that had accumulated in my absence and saw a bill from an unknown attorney, Bill Baker, for financial advice and a new will. I called his office and asked for the details of the invoice and inquired who had referred Bill to him. The secretary said that Bill had come in with Ruth Reardon.

I advised Mr. Baker that we would not need his services. Our attorney, Max Block, did not get a response from Ruth Reardon, and he suggested that we contact the assistant district attorney for elder abuse in Manhattan. Thus, started our relationship with Elizabeth Loewy, who pursued the case against Ruth Reardon.

As it turned out, Ruth Reardon had deposited the funds in Europe, so recovering them proved futile. When the DA and a detective visited Ruth Reardon, she refused to talk. Since the amount was not sufficient enough to merit a civil lawsuit, the case was not pursued. However, information was forwarded to the IRS. Elizabeth Loewy explained the extent to which the elderly are abused and pointed out that this crime was not limited to strangers but also included professional people and family members. This proved to be the case for Bill and me.

Arranging for Proper Care

An Introduction from a Caregiver's Perspective—What It Feels Like When You Have a Primary Caregiver's Role and Responsibility

> What can be worse than watching someone you love cognitively flailing until eventually they no longer recognize faces, surroundings, or even themselves?
>
> —Rudolph E. Tanzi and Ann B. Parson, *Decoding Darkness.*

One sad day, you may find that your loved one has received a diagnosis of probable Alzheimer's. Suddenly you realize that you have been transformed in the eyes of society from a regular/ordinary, featherless biped into a new sort of creature—one we call a caregiver.

Without warning, you are expected to transform yourself magically from something akin to a mythical being with superhuman attributes and virtues beyond compare. In short as a caregiver, you now are expected to possess not only the strength of Hercules but also the patience of Job and the wisdom of Solomon!

However, if you are like most caregivers, you will find this transformation quite difficult, if not impossible. No one—not even a certified saint like Mother Theresa—can meet these standards. In fact, like most people who find themselves having to assume personal responsibility for the care of a person with dementia, you will probably, at some level, resent having to assume this often thankless and surely exhausting role.

I've been there and I want to help explore some practical ways you can provide care for your loved one without totally losing your own identity or your sanity. This, of course, will necessitate your taking advantage of the many resources offered by

- Medical establishments and the professionals in the field of elder care and dementia management
- Governmental safety-net programs and entitlements for the disabled
- Alzheimer's outreach programs, such as senior-day-care centers, and various other support systems for people with dementia and their caregivers
- Volunteer programs, such as Meals on Wheels or "granny-sitting" services, offered by various community and faith groups
- Online support groups and respite programs, such as those recommended by the
- The Alzheimer's Association, as well as
- Personal and hands-on help from various family members and friends.

Other Alzheimer's caregiver issues include dealing with the loss of one's own independence and identity and one's increasing sense of isolation as the demands of caregiving grow.

At the least, we want you to know that, throughout this whole journey of caregiving, you are not alone. Many have gone before you and are willing to offer their insights about taking care of a person with dementia; many are going through what you are experiencing right now and may have helpful suggestions; and many of the younger generation may be inspired by your own caregiving example when their turn at bat comes up in the future.

From my own experience, the Alzheimer's Association is the place to go for a comprehensive overview of the entire field of dementia research and care options. In the United States, this organization is considered one of the top advocates for Alzheimer's research, funding and caregiver support, as well as an indispensable hub of information about the disease that has now become the third highest cause of mortality in the nation—right behind cancer and heart disease.

Here are a few questions and answers about this organization that might interest you.

1. What is the Alzheimer's Association?

The Alzheimer's Association is the leading voluntary health organization in Alzheimer care, support, and research. Its mission is to eliminate Alzheimer's disease through the advancement of research; to provide and enhance care and support for all affected; and to reduce the risk of dementia through the promotion of brain health.

2. What is the Alzheimer's Association website?

www.alz.org/

Do not confuse the Alzheimer's Association with the Alzheimer Foundation.

www.alzfdn.org/. They are two separate entities.

3. Why should you go to the Alzheimer's Association website first?

The Alzheimer's Association provides care and support for people with the disease, their family members and their caregivers. The association is a source of information and support and has a number of services, all of which are free.

The toll-free number is answered in English, Spanish, and Mandarin/Cantonese and translators are available in 180 languages.

Information on New York City services, including diagnostic centers, support groups and local services, such as the MedicAlert & Safe Return program, are available online at alz.orglnyc and by phone at 800-272-3900.

4. What other resources and programs does this organization offer?

The Alzheimer's Association has a twenty-four-hour help line:
1-800-272-3900.

There are chapters in all fifty states, offering myriad important services to Alzheimer patients, families, and caregivers.

For example, as of 2018, the Alzheimer's Association, New York City chapter responds to help-line callers; provides care consultations; and extends outreach activities in Russian, Chinese, African American, Latino and Orthodox Jewish communities.

5. What other organizations or groups offer services that could help Alzheimer sufferers, and their families and caregivers?

- Social: centers for seniors; YMCA, YWCA
- Adult-day-care centers
- Therapeutic programs in the visual arts, music and dance/movement
- Structured community events, interactive programs, and exhibitions
- Memory-enhancing games and programs
- Faith-based activities, support groups, and counseling
- Psychological counselors and social workers
- Professional case managers and elder-care specialists

- Books, meditation tapes, and online blogs for caregivers
- Residential facilities with special Alzheimer's units

Arranging Proper Care

Implementing Care: Some Practical Ways Caregivers Can Help
When you become a caregiver for a person with Alzheimer's, your life is changed forever. Whether you have assumed this role willingly or through default, you suddenly need to rearrange all your priorities to accommodate the needs of someone else. Now you must think for two people, one of whom is deteriorating right before your eyes.

If you are like many people who are taking on primary caregiving responsibilities, what first comes to mind may be this: How can I ever begin to anticipate all the changes that are inevitable when my loved one is caught in the tightening grip of Alzheimer's? The very thought is daunting! Yet, despite the challenge of becoming a family caregiver, you will not be doing this alone. You will find compassionate sojourners along your caretaking path to advise you about what to expect and to help you find the resources you need.

Much of this advice will most likely come first from your medical team. As you settle into a routine of structured activities, you will meet other people who have traveled the caregiving path before you. The best thing you can do right now—even while you are reading this book—is join an Alzheimer's support group. This will put you in touch with a growing network of Alzheimer's experts and other dementia caregivers who can offer practical suggestions, down-to-earth coping techniques, and emotional support.

And before you get too far down the path, I would like to gently suggest that your own well-being is just as important as that of your loved one—perhaps even more, because without you, the person with dementia would be completely at a loss. Your presence is necessary to his or her survival. And your ability to preserve your own health and sanity is necessary to your own survival. So, please take note of your own needs. Make sure you are eating well, getting enough sleep, and exercising on a regular basis. You will also need to enlist the help of others to arrange for regular time for yourself—time away from your caregiving responsibilities to recharge your own batteries, so to speak.

When someone we have known for years begins to exhibit mild cognitive impairment, with difficulties in finding words, remembering recent events, and/or dealing with ordinary activities of living, it is often difficult not to be judgmental. If someone repeats the same story, or forgets where household things belong, or loses his or her way in the grocery store, it may be tempting for us to chide or lose our patience. For caregivers of people with dementia, a good sense of humor and a flexible approach go a long way.

In their compassionate book entitled *A Dignified Life: The Best Friends Approach to Alzheimer's Care*, Virginia Bell and David Troxel suggest gentle ways of dealing with a cognitively impaired loved one, using what they call knack. Knack has been defined variously as skill (an easy and smart way of doing something or handling a problem) and

natural ability (a particular skill, especially one that might be innate or intuitive and therefore difficult to teach).

Knack in the context of caregiving may be thought of as that undefinable attitude that preserves another person's dignity, while at the same time communicating a message that needs to be conveyed. The use of knack as an interpersonal communications strategy in Alzheimer's caregiving requires, among other things, such skills and attributes as

- Good listening
- Empathy
- Humor
- Creativity
- Patience

Moreover, in addition to the previously mentioned attributes, when dealing with a person who is trying to cope with a loss in cognitive acuity, it is important for caregivers to observe the following guidelines:

- Don't argue. A person with dementia cannot reason logically.

6. Arranging for Proper Care

An argument will only add to his or her frustration and may lead to inappropriate behavior.

- Be affectionate. A hug says more than words to someone who is already afraid and insecure.

- Keep to a routine. The familiarity of a predictable routine creates a greater sense of security for a person experiencing memory loss and disorientation.

- Use repetition. Try different ways of saying the same thing. One of them might get through the thicket of plaques and tangles that are clouding your loved one's mind.

- Use nonverbal ways of communicating—try to convey your message with your voice levels and inflections, as well with as your facial expressions, gestures, and body language.

- Treat the person as an adult, not a child. Try not to raise your voice in frustration or talk down to the person.

- Respond to emotional needs. Acknowledge feelings that your loved one may have difficulties in expressing.

- Be aware of the importance of timing. For instance, leave extra time to get ready for appointments and don't make a demanding request when someone is going through a period of sundowning.

- Screen out upsetting news or information. There is enough anxiety associated with dementia without adding more fuel to the fire. Use your best judgment in dealing with bad news. For instance, the death of a spouse or other loved one may require special handing, depending on the stage of memory loss. A person with mild cognitive impairment certainly needs to be told of a family loss and will comprehend what has happened. He or she is capable of feeling genuine grief and being in need of comforting. But someone who is at a much later stage of Alzheimer's may not be able to even comprehend such a loss.

- Help-out with hints to jog memory and find lost words. Sometimes your ability to voice the right word will give your loved one a feeling of greater security and less isolation.

- Help your loved one, who is already feeling confused, save face. A person struggling with memory loss and disorientation can suffer greatly from a loss of self-esteem. As a primary caregiver, you can look for ways to say, "Yes, that's right," or turn a potentially embarrassing situation around for your loved one.

- Turn "no" into "yes" by diverting, distracting, and reframing.

- Coping with constant confusion is exhausting for a person with Alzheimer's and creates an ongoing situation which can lead to resistance and other negative behaviors.

- *Note*: These behaviors often become problematic during travel to and from medical appointments and at mealtime and bedtime. Other occasions that can trigger recalcitrance on the part of your loved one frequently occur when prophylactic bathroom breaks are suggested or when you insist that taking a bath is not something to be put off any longer.

- Encourage the person to remember. Long-term memories are usually more accessible to people with Alzheimer's than short-term memories. Playing old favorites and other familiar music has been shown to help cognitively compromised individuals access pleasant memories and even spontaneously participate in singing and/or dancing.

- Structure activities for your loved one, try to tap into

remaining physical skills. As a caregiver, you will need to be creative in modifying standard exercise routines and games to accommodate your loved one's level of stamina and ability to stay focused. For example, an older person with progressive dementia might not be able to participate in a real game of volleyball, but he or she could perhaps engage in a gently paced game of catch using a large light-weight ball.

- Use heartfelt communication to connect with your loved one and include him or her in family life. A person with Alzheimer's may often feel marginalized and left out. Whenever you convey genuine acceptance and affection to your loved one, your efforts can go a long way to enhance the quality of life for the person in your care.

- Case in point: People with mild to moderate cognitive impairment may enjoy interacting with young grandchildren and pets. Of course, all such interactions should be lovingly supervised. People with Alzheimer's may tire easily or become anxious and start pacing around nervously. A good caregiver will monitor the level of fatigue their loved one is experiencing and provide for naps and/or quite times to compensate for these expected challenges.

- Lighten up! Try to keep your own spirits up as you seek to bolster those of your loved one.

Whatever you do to set up a safe and supportive caregiving environment, it is still important to keep in mind how your loved one might be feeling from moment to moment. For us as caregivers, however difficult it may seem at times, it is imperative to remember that a person with Alzheimer's is still a person, to paraphrase Horton the elephant's motto in Dr. Seuss's beloved children's book *Horton Hatches the Egg*. This phrase should become a caregiver's mantra.

More than anything else we caregivers can offer, it is our loving and responsible attitude—our willingness to care, our determination to be there when the going gets tough, and our commitment to remain faithful to the task we have undertaken—that is most needed. Our physically vulnerable, mentally confused, and frightened loved one who, through no fault of his or her own, is suffering from one of the most devastating diseases ever to exist on this planet deserves at all times to be treated with dignity and compassion.

The changes that go along with Alzheimer's can make caring for a loved one with the disease difficult. Because Alzheimer's, the most common type of dementia, is a progressive illness that causes irreversible brain damage, these changes can be frightening for both the caregiver and the person with Alzheimer's.

Recognizing that the life-changing symptoms of Alzheimer's are caused by the disease and not the person you're caring for is often the first step to becoming a compassionate and effective caregiver. Finding new ways to approach your loved one's needs can also help you handle your ever-changing role.

Forget about the Memory Lapses
Lapses in memory are one of the first symptoms of Alzheimer's, and they occur with greater frequency and severity as the disease progresses. There's no point in arguing about them or trying to make the person remember. Just change the subject.

Find Things You Both Enjoy Every Day
Every caregiver has an individual style of caregiving, much as people have their own parenting or fashion styles. The challenge is to recognize your individual style and find a way to take care of your own needs as well as your loved one's so you can both do the things you enjoy. For example, a caregiver who's focused on meeting emotional needs may enjoy turning bathing into a spa experience, with hand and foot massages, soothing music, or aromatherapy.

Other types of caregivers may want to hire someone to come in and take care of the bathing so they can devote their energies to other activities, like cooking or managing medical care.

One recommended exercise to help caregivers make choices about daily activities is to create a spreadsheet with caregiving priorities in the first column and the interests of the care recipient in the top row. Then fill the cells in between with possibilities for activities where the two intersect.

Once you've narrowed down your activities, you can create a daily plan. Having a daily routine allows you to spend less time each day figuring out what to do and more time enjoying activities that provide a feeling of fulfillment for both of you.

Keep Things Simple
When planning a daily routine, try to keep tasks as familiar as possible. Things stored in the procedural memory, like brushing hair or teeth, are often easier for people with Alzheimer's to remember than other tasks are.

People with Alzheimer's often get confused or forget how to use modern tools like electric toothbrushes or kitchen appliances. But their long-term procedural memory may still function for other, simpler items used in the past.

Think about what kind of objects the person with Alzheimer's used at an earlier time. Some detective work may be involved to figure out what is most familiar.

The simple act of replacing an electric toothbrush with a manual one or an electric mixer with a hand beater may allow people with Alzheimer's to continue to perform many tasks of daily living on their own.

Stay Active Together
Physical activity can help both the person with Alzheimer's and the caregiver feel better in general.

People with Alzheimer's disease who exercise at least one hour twice a week, either in a group or at home with a caregiver, experience fewer falls and a slower rate of decline in physical function than those who don't exercise. You can stay active together by

- Taking a walk every day
- Adding music and dancing to your exercise routine if your

loved one enjoys music

- Using exercise videos or DVDs designed for older people
- Gardening
- Walking a dog

It's hard to say scientifically whether these things provide any benefits, but many experts agree: there's little downside to such activities.

The Internet: Online Support, Innovative Technologies, and New Approaches to Care

Technology has changed how we get information: "Just Google it" is a phrase many of us use every day and a Google search reveals information on most subjects, including medicine. "Google" has even become a verb!

The internet has revolutionized the way we communicate and the way business is transacted. It has also changed how we access medical research and, most recently, how clinical medicine is practiced. Recently, the University of California–San Francisco and the University of Nebraska Medical Center received a $10 million grant to create a web-based model for dementia care. This model, called a Dementia Care Ecosystem, will provide twenty-four-hour consultation for patients and their families, web-based education and, for some patients, remote monitoring with the use of smart phones and other devices.

Other technologies include Balance, a dementia-care app for use by family members, medical professionals, and caregivers on iPhones, iPads, and computers. In New York, the Hebrew Home for the Aged in Riverdale and its family of services conduct research and created the award-winning Balance program for family members caring for someone with Alzheimer's. For a one-time fee of ninety-nine cents, one can obtain the Balance app, which can be used worldwide. It was developed by David Pomeranz and his team at the Hebrew Home and is designed to help family members communicate with each other.

Another Hebrew Home service is the ElderServe at Night program, which is designed primarily to give caregivers some rest and provide care and

6. Arranging for Proper Care

appropriate activities for dementia victims. It is a sleep-over for both. Caregivers' sleep deprivation is often the reason families seek nursing homes for the person with Alzheimer's.

In response to the urgent and overwhelming need to reverse sleep deprivation in Alzheimer's caregivers, this innovative and ground-breaking respite program offers dementia patients such varied options as listening to music, dancing, and resting, as well as participating in sing-alongs, crafts, and even therapy sessions. And it offers these services at an hour when most people are usually sound asleep. As sundowning is usual in those with dementia, this is a welcome aid to families and a lifesaver to exhausted caregivers.

The Hebrew Home is unique and has one location for inpatient care but offers many other services. The process and cost to be able to participate in these programs can be obtained from their webpage, or by telephone at 1-800-567-3676.

The Hebrew Home at Riverdale has approximately one thousand people in residence and provides in-home nursing care for another ten thousand people, with the same services as offered in the residential program for the aging. The Hebrew Home and the Visiting Nurse Association (VNA) of New York are key providers of nursing home care in New York City. Besides providing care, the Hebrew Home has a research and educational facility that assures their services are delivered by skilled and talented people. Innovative and unique programs they have developed offer free on-site training and assistance to doormen, concierges, porters, and other building staff across New York City to look out for abuse of elderly residents. They have focused on educating people who work with or around the elderly, such as estate lawyers, bank tellers, therapists, and delivery people.

The Weinberg Center for Elder Abuse Prevention at the Hebrew Home provide emergency shelter for victims of elder abuse and promotes enhanced public awareness and knowledge of elder abuse. The shelter has a full-range of health care and supporting services that include psychological counseling, legal advocacy, and representation of victims of elder abuse. The toll-free number to call for assistance, referral, or setting up a community outreach program is 1-800-567-3646. More than fifty-two thousand people have been helped by this program.

The Hebrew Home has both day and night programs on-site. The day program offers five hours of a safe, stimulating environment for seniors to socialize and exercise, and alternative therapies. Caregivers must bring the person to the home. The night program is from seven p.m. to seven a.m. and provides transportation to and from the home. Seniors can have a bed for sleeping or may take part in social and recreational activities. Assistance is available for bathing, grooming, and eating. Unfortunately, the number of people that can be accommodated is only thirty-six.

The Hebrew Home's innovative ElderServe at Night program has helped save the sanity of untold sleep-deprived families of Alzheimer's patients. It is a dusk-to-dawn drop-off program intended to strengthen their decaying minds while sating their thirst to be active after dark.

Skype is another technological advancement that can enhance access to caregiving support and medical input through the internet. A connection is made via a telephone—a call online—and participants have a virtual face-to-face experience talking with the other person (or persons) whose face and voice appear simultaneously on the computer screen, thus providing visual and auditory as well as personal and interactive communication in real time.

Psychiatry and Alzheimer's: Who Needs a Psychiatrist, Why, and When?

As the importance of mental-health issues has gained increasing recognition over the course of the last century and is now considered less a stigma among the general public than it once was, many people have relied on the help of a psychiatrist during stressful periods of their lives. In this age of anxiety, seeking psychiatric help for marital problems, personal issues, and other anxiety-producing situations has become socially acceptable. In fact, in certain sophisticated circles, having a "shrink" is considered a status symbol.

In light of these changing societal attitudes, seeking the help of a psychiatrist—that is, a physician who is an expert in the combined fields of medicine, psychopharmacology, and mental-health counseling—when one is facing overwhelming life challenges is a wise decision for anyone. And when those challenges threaten to wipe out one's entire memory bank, distort one's personality beyond recognition, and eventually deprive one of life itself, the decision to seek professional psychiatric help is all the more critical.

From a family caregiver's perspective, it is easy to imagine that anyone who is about to experience the onset of early Alzheimer's would be prone to suffer high anxiety upon hearing his or her diagnosis. As caregivers, we should strive to be as empathetic to the emotional state of our loved one with incipient Alzheimer's as we are concerned with his or her other medical issues. We should be willing to seek the same level of professional expertise to address the psychological, spiritual, and existential distress as we would to address our loved one's physical needs.

People with early-stage Alzheimer's often find themselves facing symptoms of uncertainty about the future and doubts about their ability to cope with this stressful period of their lives. Despite cognitive decline serious enough to warrant an Alzheimer's diagnosis, many people in the early to mid stages of the disease suffer immense grief over their impending fate. Clinical depression is not uncommon. Yet there is still hope for dealing with the inevitable trajectory of the disease, with its concomitant loss of mental and physical function as well as ultimately the disintegration of self.

In speaking with Dr. Dimitris N. Kiosses of the Department of Psychiatry, Weil-Cornell Institute of Geriatric Psychiatry, Weill Medical College of Cornell University, New York, I learned that people with mild to moderate Alzheimer's disease symptoms can be helped to achieve a more productive life through psychiatric consultation. At the same time, the person with Alzheimer's disease is confronting the diagnosis, the caregiver is facing a lifestyle change as well. According to a recent article in the *Whole Heath Insider* entitled "Caregivers in Crisis," 61 percent of Alzheimer's caregivers say they're under high stress. Caregiving is stressful. It's isolating. And it's emotionally and physically draining. But it's hard for most people to imagine that caring for a sick or disabled loved one could actually be deadly. How can this be? you might ask. To answer this question, it may be wise to explore a number of precipitating factors that can negatively affect caregivers and their stress levels.

First of all, the length of time that Alzheimer's resides in the individual with the disease creates a devastating period of sheer agony for the primary caregiver and the individual alike. Unlike other diseases, like cancer, that may have a prolonged period of illness, Alzheimer's presents a unique combination of symptoms that may vary from medical to mental, ultimately resulting in strangers facing each other as the disease progresses.

Against this bleak backdrop, we may begin to realize the heavy toll that Alzheimer's caregiving can take on your health. Below are a few noteworthy observations about the health risks that caretaking involves:

- Caregivers are much more likely to struggle with depression, and up to 70 percent of caregivers are clinically depressed.
- People caring for relatives with dementia tend to pay the highest price.
- Stress and anxiety among caregivers are often linked with hostility, self-medication, and self-harm.
- Caregivers tend to neglect their own physical health.
- Caregivers report chronic health conditions at twice the rate of non-caregivers.
- They have a greater propensity to serious illness and infection, as wells as other stress-induced health issues such as obesity, pain, reflux, headaches, blood-sugar imbalances, and digestive problems.
- Caregivers are more vulnerable to cardiovascular problems such as high blood pressure and heart disease.
- Stressed-out older caregivers face a higher risk of death from any cause.

In fact, caregiving may actually double the risk of death. And when you combine the day- to-day stress from caregiving itself with the external stress from other sources—such as family power struggles and unscrupulous people waiting to prey upon the helpless state of someone suffering from dementia, then you may start to see a crisis of potentially volcanic proportions.

This is when and where the expertise of a psychiatrist—a caring physician grounded in medicine but acutely aware of the psychology of stress, exhaustion, and grief—can be helpful.

For without a caregiver, the Alzheimer's patient is left adrift in a world that grows more frightening each day as the disease progresses. Alzheimer's caregivers need to recognize their own needs in order to survive an ordeal of virtually seismic magnitude. It is not an admission of defeat to seek help from an expert in mental and physical health when you are under the very threat of an early demise yourself. It is not an admission of weakness to realize that you as a caregiver need to talk about your own frustrations, issues, and fears as well as those of your loved one. And sometimes we all need to learn how to set limits more effectively to ensure our own survival as we face the inevitable downward spiral of Alzheimer's disease.

Who better to help us than an expert in mental health? Is it really too much to ask for emotional and spiritual support on behalf of oneself? Would taking a beta blocker or other anxiety-reducing medication not help you better cope with the relentless stress you as a caregiver are under? Are you not entitled to consideration and some moments of relaxation and personal freedom?

Recognition of the value of one's own sacrifice and validation of one's altruistic motives in caring for another human being are responses we all need to hear. And is it not possible that when such validation comes from someone in a position of authority and respect it can be all the more meaningful?

If you find yourself fighting with depression and on the verge of despair, do not hesitate to take yourself seriously. Your very life and that of the one you care for are at stake and may very well depend on your willingness to seek psychiatric help for yourself as well as for your loved one.

Choosing the Medical Team: Finding the Health Care

Professionals and Providers Your Loved One Needs

Choosing the medical team is a very individual choice based on the circumstances of the person with Alzheimer's and the family or the primary caregiver. I have listed the types of health care people one generally needs and described how to provide for appointments. Each person will have to select who and when each is needed.

Different types of health care professionals and providers are needed to diagnose, treat, and manage care for Alzheimer's patients.

Doctors

- Neurologist who specializes in diseases of the brain and nervous system
- Psychiatrist who specializes in disorders that affect mood or the way the mind works
- Psychologist with special training in testing memory and other mental functions
- Gerontologist (if needed) who specializes in diagnosing and treating conditions common in older patients
- Other physicians (if needed) who are specialists in diagnosing and treating concomitant conditions such as diabetes, heart disease, kidney problems, gastro-intestinal and swallowing issues, as well as pain management and palliative care at the end stage, as needed.

Case Managers

- Social worker
- Adult-day-care manager
- In-town care manager for long-distance caregivers

6. Arranging for Proper Care

Therapists

- Physical therapist
- Occupational therapist
- Speech therapist
- Music/art therapist

Nursing and Caregiving Providers

- Skilled nurses
- Nutritionists
- Respiratory technicians
- Home health aides
- Hospice care staff

How can you prepare for doctor appointments and evaluations of your loved one?

1. Bring a list of all medications and supplements (vitamins, protein drinks, and so on).

2. Bring a list of symptoms your loved one is displaying. Describe how things have changed from when you first noticed symptoms to those occurring for the first time between office visits.

3. Prepare a complete medical history, with dates of vaccines and other inoculations, trips to exotic places with possible exposure to pathogens, known childhood diseases and major illnesses and/or injuries, chronic health conditions, mental-health issues, and surgical procedures.

4. Compile a list of known allergies, including negative

reactions to foods and certain medications, such as antibiotics and psychotropic drugs.

5. Bring a list of questions you have about medical issues that concern you.

6. Keep a calendar of medical appointments and update frequently.

7. Arrange transportation to and from consultations and evaluation sessions with plenty of advanced leeway to take into consideration the additional stress that traveling may create for your loved one.

8. Try to establish cordial working relationships with your loved one's medical team. Coordinate meetings so that each member of the team has timely and accurate information from the other team members about any changes in the health or mental status of your loved one.

9. Don't be afraid to ask for explanations of medical issues in lay terms.

10. Keep notes about the meetings.

11. Organize the patient's day according to treatment protocols.

12. Keep close track of all medications and supplements taken by your loved one.

13. Work with doctors, nurses, and nutritionists to insure proper nourishment.

14. Ask about sundowning, sleep issues (reversal of day and night), and wandering.

15. Don't be embarrassed to bring up such topics as inappropriate sexual behavior and elder abuse.

16. Ask about how to protect the one you care for in terms of driving, home safety, and tracking someone who wanders and is likely to get lost.

17. Ask your social worker or other care coordinator for referrals to ongoing emotional and caregiving support for yourself.

18. Be sure to keep up with your own medical appointments. As a primary caregiver you could now be at a higher risk for stress-induced disease yourself.

Choosing a Nursing Home: When Home Care Becomes Overwhelming for You as a Caregiver and Other Care Options You May Consider

Choosing a nursing home is a difficult task and a time-consuming process involving financial, emotional, and medical concerns. One should start investigating options sooner rather than later, as choices may be limited due to each individual situation.

I chose the Franke Home in Mount Pleasant, South Carolina, as it had different levels of care and was near to friends and family, who initially visited the site multiple times to see the environment and observe the staff. It was a wonderful choice, offering clean and attractive rooms, a well-trained and diverse caring staff, and a variety of activities. The staff was friendly and open to questions and seemed to enjoy their work.

The Alzheimer's Association is a resource to help locate accredited facilities (www.alz.org/visitinganursinghome.pdf). If you are working with a social worker, they usually can help you select the best fit for your needs.

There are many reasons for choosing to place one who is suffering with dementia in a skilled-nursing facility, such as sleep deprivation on the part of the caregiver. Many family members want to care for relatives with Alzheimer's at home, but, in order to do that, the caregivers themselves have to remain healthy. You cannot stay healthy if you don't get a good night's sleep.

But no matter what the precipitating reason, when you and your family finally reach the point of needing to place your loved one in a nursing home, there are several questions you should try to keep in mind as you consider your options. There are three vital questions to ask first:

1. Does the home have a current license from the state?

2. Does the administrator have a current license from the state?

3. Does the home meet or exceed state fire regulations? Because it is difficult to evacuate frail elderly people in case of fire, sprinkler systems and fire doors are important.

If any of these questions cannot be answered yes, do not use the home. Other important questions to ask include the following:

1. Is the home certified to accept Medicare or Medicaid?

2. Is there a written contract setting forth the agreed date of admission and the care to be furnished?

3. Under what conditions could the resident be asked to leave (decline in health, behavioral symptoms, problems walking, incontinence)?

4. How much notice must the facility give you?

5. If the patient's condition changes, will the home move him or her? And if so, will it be to another part of the same home?

Finding a place that suits the needs of an aging relative or friend, and those who plan to visit, requires considerable preparation. The biggest mistake people make is waiting until the last minute, when faced with a crisis, to find a suitable facility. Then you're forced into an impulsive decision that you're not likely to be happy with unless you're really very lucky.

Once you have decided to explore the options available to choose a nursing home, you then must figure out where to start.

Searching for a new residence for a dementia-compromised relative or friend is not exactly something people are accustomed to doing on a regular basis. In fact, many people feel an aversion to the whole idea of placing a person in an "institution." We all either know or have heard of someone who felt honor-bound to fulfill an unrealistic and perhaps extorted promise not to put a loved one into a home—no matter what. With that kind of guilt, it is more than difficult to begin the process of looking around and assessing what situation might be best. Yet, at some point—preferably sooner rather than later—begin you must.

One place to start is with the cost. You need to know that Medicare does not pay for long-term nursing home care, only for short-term rehabilitative stays. If the patient does not have long-term-care insurance, then costs must be paid out of pocket—that is, unless the patient qualifies for Medicaid and the institution accepts assignment, in which case, most of the cost is covered. Of course, there are stringent requirements that must be met for the patient to become a Medicaid beneficiary. The patient must be

- Disabled
- A U.S. citizen
- Have no more than a certain amount of assets

If the patient does not qualify for Medicaid, you are looking at a monthly nursing home expense of $10,000 to $15,000. If a transfer of assets to a third party was made at least five years prior to admission, then the person might become eligible for Medicaid coverage. The exact rules and regulations for Medicaid qualification should be discussed with a social worker or other expert in elder-care law, as it varies from state to state.

Another important consideration is location. The facility you choose should be relatively convenient for the most frequent visitors. Access via public transportation may be a priority or not. Also, if you live near another state or even another country, you might want to explore cost differentials relative to each option. One friend I know who was primary caregiver for her Alzheimer's-stricken life partner decided to take him back to his native Canada because he was a Canadian citizen and therefore eligible for government-underwritten nursing home care. She commuted by train from New York City to Montreal every weekend to visit him. However, if at all possible, you don't want to have to deal with difficult transportation problems that might preclude you from visiting as often as you would like.

Narrow down your search to a particular area or ZIP code. Then you should make a list of the various nursing homes in that vicinity and check out their ratings. There is a governmental report card assessing every skilled-nursing facility that receives federal funding. Choose only those institutions with a rating above 3, on a scale of 1 to 5.

Narrow down your search by specialized services offered. Memory units or dementia-care programs, as well as any nearby hospital affiliations or personally known physicians who have privileges at the institution. Culture- or language-affiliated residential facilities are another consideration, especially if your loved one is not fluent in English.

Take a tour and make a list of quality-of-life and quality-of-care factors. Don't be misled by brochures. Visit several times, and at different hours of the day and night, including mealtime. Note the smells, level of cleanliness, and personalization allowed in individual rooms, as well as staff friendliness, knowledge of each patient, and turnover rate. Check out the menu, list of rules and regulations, and flexibility or rigidity in accommodating individual residents' needs. Other issues to check off on your list include quality of life, quality of care, safety, nutrition, and hydration.

Speak with management and/or supervising staff members about any special needs of your loved one. Take down names and keep dated and detailed notes of your meetings. Find out the protocol for addressing complaints.

Set up health proxies and make sure you have access to the patient's medical records.

6. Arranging for Proper Care

Frequently monitor the care that the patient is receiving. Check for any signs of physical abuse or neglect, such as hidden bruises and bedsores.

Besides avoiding nursing facilities with negative aspects—such as the pervasive smell of urine, the employment of physical restraints, the overuse of sedatives to control patient behavior, and a high rate of staff turnover, it is important for families to choose a facility that offers many positive aspects to enhance their loved one's comfort and care.

One aspect is certainly the availability of different levels of care. As dementia patients progress through the various stages of Alzheimer's disease, for example, their needs change, often dramatically. What once may have been perceived by an Alzheimer's patient as a pleasantly stimulating activity may now be perceived as overwhelming or even frightening. As the disease continues its relentless destruction of neurons, people with advancing dementia may become more disoriented and anxious, they may exhibit aggressive and other inappropriate behaviors, and they may need to move around more to discharge excess and unfocused energy. Often they may even attempt to wander from the premises. A good nursing home should be able to accommodate all these levels of patient need. Just because a facility has a bona fide memory unit does not mean that it is necessarily equipped to accommodate the changing needs of the residential dementia patients.

Before deciding on a particular nursing home, family members should ascertain how other patients at various levels seem to respond to their surroundings. Are there exercise programs and supervised involvement in physical interaction? Is pet therapy allowed? What about the availability of art, music, dance, and singing therapy? Many patients respond to personalized music therapy when they can no longer respond verbally.

As caregivers, we must never lose sight of the fact that our loved one, however challenged by Alzheimer's, is still a human being worthy of the same level of respect and consideration afforded to patients with other medical conditions. A lost memory found in a familiar song can bring back a sense of joy often missing in the life of a person with progressive dementia. And a nursing home that addresses the emotional needs of its residents as well as their medical needs is one certainly to be commended.

Once you have settled on a particular nursing home, you hope that you can finally breathe a sigh of relief and get some sleep! You certainly deserve the respite, and the person with Alzheimer's disease deserves the best care. Unfortunately, however, even when a person with Alzheimer's is securely housed in a skilled-care facility (one with perhaps a memory unit as well), it is still incumbent upon caregivers and families to monitor their care. Incidents of substandard care, medical malpractice, and even elder abuse abound in many facilities that, although equipped with state-of the art technology and luxury hotel-like decor, are often plagued with high staff burn-out and turnover, second-rate administrators who are more concerned with the bottom line than with the quality of patient care, and overworked doctors who may not take the time needed for in-depth individualized patient follow-up.

Officials at the Centers for Medicare and Medicaid Services, which runs Medicare, say the rating system is supposed to give nursing homes an incentive to improve, but many nursing homes have found ways to game the system. They often know when inspectors will show up and add workers just beforehand and sharply cut staff immediately afterward. And the quality data compiled by the nursing homes themselves such as how many patients develop bedsores or experience serious falls, is obviously subject to manipulation.

The Affordable Care Act requires Medicare to use payroll data to verify staff levels, but the agency is still working on such a verification system. Medicare should also spot-check the quality statistics while developing a broader auditing program. Improvements are clearly necessary—and we need them soon because Medicare is about to introduce similar five-star ratings for hospitals, dialysis centers, and home health care agencies.

The Medicare ratings, which have become the gold standard across the industry, are based in large part on self-reported data by the nursing homes, and the government does not verify it. Only one of the three criteria used to determine the star ratings—the results of annual health inspections—relies on assessments from independent reviewers. The other measures—staff levels and quality statistics—are reported by the nursing homes and accepted by

6. Arranging for Proper Care

Medicare, with limited exceptions, at face value. The few that I personally visited varied so much that I suggest you have to make your own decision after at least two or three unannounced visits.

According to a *Frontline* expose entitled "Death in Assisted Living," which aired on public television in 2013, the situation is even worse in the case of assisted-living facilities. These facilities are often glorified hotel-like residences with no safeguards for dementia patients who may—as has happened in the past—wander away and get lost, fall out of a window and break a bone, or unwittingly ingest unsecured cleaning fluids and die. Unlike certified nursing homes, which bear legal responsibility for securing and monitoring the well-being and medical status of their residents, assisted-living facilities often include medical nonliability clauses in their contracts.

The televised presentation points out the vast difference between assisted-living and nursing home care—a difference that is especially relevant to those caregivers and families whose loved one is suffering from Alzheimer's disease or another dementia. The following information was also brought to light in the PBS documentary:

- Assisted living is less regulated than nursing homes, and there is no limitation on the fees charged.

- Assisted-living institutions now house a population of not well elderly: many are in wheelchairs and use walkers; many (some two-thirds of assisted-living residents) have Alzheimer's disease and/or other cognitive impairments.

- Memory-care facilities, as dementia and Alzheimer's units are called, are now being opened in unprecedented numbers.

- One reason is that facilities can charge more for these special units (which feature rooms around a courtyard but no special training for staff who must deal with such compromised residents; all they are given is the minimum training of one eight-hour orientation class).

- Ten years ago, nonwell residents who now find themselves in assisted-living facilities were in nursing homes.

The attitudes expressed by some executives and administrators of assisted-living facilities who were interviewed in the PBS documentary were appalling and would give anyone who is considering placing one with dementia into an assisted-living facility great cause for concern. Below are a few excerpts describing policies and practices promulgated at Emeritus, one exceptionally large chain of assisted-living facilities throughout the United States:

> "Fill the buildings!" was the policy of Emeritus. Despite an "Ethics" hotline, many employee caregivers were fired for reporting abuses and shortcomings in staffing and care protocols. According to some former employees, Corporate pushed for more money to increase cash flow by targeting seriously ill seniors but not hiring enough competent staff or directors required under state law, and even under Emeritus's own standards. The Memory Care director at one facility didn't have the required training and background for her position. "Cut labor expenses. Don't use commonly recognized patient/staffing ratios." These were the stated corporate directives. Another policy, "Keep the back door shut," was meant to ensure that no one ever moved out of an Emeritus facility before they died.

Considering the widespread naiveté of most caregivers today about the dangers inherent for severely compromised patients who have been placed in assisted-living facilities rather than in nursing homes, we must take note of one particularly alarming demographic projection from the documentary before making a decision about any kind of institutional care for those with Alzheimer's:

there are currently more than 1 million Americans in assisted-living facilities, and a huge increase in this population is expected over the next fifteen to twenty years, as the baby boomer generation ages.

For patients with Alzheimer's and other dementias who are being assigned to the wrong type of care facility—either by well-meaning but unwitting family members or by unscrupulous placement agents—the implications are frightening. And the repercussions of ignorance on a caregiver's part can lead to the suffering and premature death of the very person to whom they have dedicated their caretaking efforts.

As one exposé after another continues to bring to light more and more of the egregious practices found in the growing adult-care industry in this country, the answer is becoming increasingly apparent to the already-stressed-out population of caregivers. When it comes to choosing institutional care for your Alzheimer's-impaired loved one, the old adage Caveat emptor (Let the buyer beware) must be applied with all due diligence. This warning is not merely a hackneyed suggestion; it is nothing less than a matter of life and death.

Common Issues in Institutional Settings: What to Do When You Suspect Patient Neglect and/or Elder Abuse

While most people may think that elder abuse occurs primarily in institutional settings, the unfortunate reality is that most incidents of elder abuse occur in the home and are perpetrated by those closest to the older person:

Elder abuse is on the rise in America, especially as the huge baby boomer generation is now reaching retirement age. According to Sy Moskowitz, a professor of law at Valparaiso Law School in Indiana who specializes in elder law and elder abuse and neglect, "Experts estimate that there are 1.5 million to 2 million cases of elder abuse a year in the U.S., but that only 5 percent to 10 percent are reported to authorities."

According to the Alzheimer's Association and Professor Moskowitz, "Older adults with Alzheimer's and other forms of dementia are especially vulnerable. They're less able to prevent these kinds of abusive situations, and they have less access to outsiders. Elder abuse can have dire consequences. The fact is, elder abuse and neglect is a big risk factor for death. It can even lead to suicide." There are a number of ways that elder abuse can manifest. Here are some of them:

- Physical abuse may involve hitting, shoving, and inflicting pain on the older adult.

- Verbal abuse may include yelling, threatening, or ridiculing the elderly person.

- Psychological abuse may involve ignoring the elderly person, isolating him or her from others, or menacing the victim.

- Sexual abuse is engaging the elderly person in inappropriate sexual activities.

- Financial exploitation involves the misuse of the elderly person's money without his or her consent. It may involve forgery, theft, or inappropriate use of the elder's credit cards and checking accounts.

- Neglect can mean failing to meet the elderly person's most basic needs, whether food, water, or clothing. It may also be withholding medication or isolating him or her from others.

Many cases of elder abuse never get reported to authorities. Victims are often too intimidated or embarrassed to turn in the abuser and may not want them to get in trouble. There may also be a lot of fear, as in, "Who is going to take care of me if I turn them in?"

While there is no typical profile of someone who commits elder abuse, certain factors do raise the risk for abuse: many people who abuse the elderly are frustrated, stressed caregivers.

Like most forms of domestic violence, it isn't always easy to spot an elderly victim of abuse, especially if you don't see that person on a regular basis. But, there are clues that sometimes may cause concern. Victims who are being physically hurt, for instance, may have unexplained bruises, broken bones, or other inexplicable injuries. Those who are being neglected may lose weight, become increasingly isolated, and disappear from activities that they once cherished.

Financial abuse is tougher to spot, especially if you don't have access to the victim's accounts. But if you do, you may notice large, unexplained withdrawals of cash from bank accounts, changes in her financial situation, unpaid bills, and suspicious changes in documents such as wills, power of attorney, and insurance policies.

Even so, many cases of elder abuse are so subtle as to go unseen. For instance, an unemployed child may simply "borrow" funds from an elderly parent with the intention of paying it back someday, or an exhausted caregiver may grab the elderly person's arm when she refuses to cooperate.

And in the current economic climate, experts say the incidence of financial abuse has gone up. Of particular concern is a caregiver with power of attorney over an elderly parent's assets and finances, especially when there is evidence of financial mismanagement.

Preventing Abuse

For caregivers, the best thing they can do to stop themselves from becoming abusers is to be aware of the fragility of their situation and to look out for their own well-being. Here's what experts advise caregivers to do to avoid slipping into an abusive situation:

- Join a support group. Local organizations such as the Alzheimer's Association often provide weekly support groups for caregivers to gather and talk about the challenges of caregiving. Being with others in your situation can be a tremendous source of comfort and relief.

- Take advantage of community services. These organizations—which may be agencies, churches, or local nonprofits—are also often able to help with practical care. Some provide adult day care and respite services to give caregivers breaks.

- Stay socially connected. It's easy to abandon friends and social activities when you're in the throes of caregiving. But maintaining connections can help caregivers endure the difficulties.

- Do what's necessary to stay healthy. Exercise, a good night's sleep, and healthy meals aren't luxuries—they're necessities for well-being.

- Be smart with your time. Caregivers should know their limitations, learn to make lists of what needs to be done, and do what they can to make the best of their time. Even knowing the layout of the store when shopping for groceries can save time and make a caregiver less fretful.

- Learn to ask for help. Resist the urge to do everything all by yourself. Instead, delegate responsibilities to siblings, your children, your spouse, and others. If no one wants to help, ask for contributions of money instead. Use the money to hire someone for a couple hours or days while you take a break.

- Talk to a professional. If you think you're on the brink of becoming abusive, seek professional help from a therapist or social worker. Airing your concerns can relieve stress and help you regain your footing while avoiding an abusive situation.

Here's what you can do if you think someone is being victimized:

- If you think an elderly person is being abused, contact your state's Adult Protective Services agency or the police. You can also locate help on the National Center on Elder Abuse website at www.ncea.aoa.gov.

- If you don't live near the victim, you can contact the national Eldercare Locator number to find services and agencies in the community where the victim lives. That number is 1-800-677-1116.

- And if you're the victim of elder abuse, consider reporting it to the police or talking to your physician, a clergy member, or a close friend. They may be able to report the problem and get you the help you need. Remember, elder abuse is a crime.

6. Arranging for Proper Care

Human/Senior Sexuality in Institutional Settings: How to Deal with a Taboo Subject

Baby boomers burned their bras and developed the pill. Do we really think they're not going to be sexual as they age?"

In her 2007 *New York Times* article entitled "Love in the Time of Dementia," which recounts Supreme Court Justice Sandra Day O'Connor's unusual and poignant reaction to the nursing home romance her Alzheimer's-afflicted husband was having with another woman, Kate Zernike writes: "The former justice is thrilled—even visits with the new couple while they hold hands on the porch swing—because it is a relief to see her husband of 55 years so content."

Yet such compassionate responses to overt displays of affection on the part of the elderly are not always the case.

Nursing homes and other care-giving institutions are facing increasingly complex problems in the area of senior sexuality, especially for patients with Alzheimer's and other dementias, many of whom have lost their ability to understand social norms and behave accordingly or to consent to sexual relations.

It is commonly acknowledged that people are sexually active well into their seventies and eighties. For those with dementia, intimacy and sex can be a healthy comfort as they lose comprehension of family and friends. Federal and state laws require care facilities to respect residents' rights to privacy, including for kissing, fondling, intercourse, and other sexual activity. Yet for many elder-care facilities and residential institutions across the U.S., these laws have not been adequately translated into policies and protocols designed to address the specific needs and problems presented by their patients with dementia.

To asked what can be done to alleviate a patient's isolation and preserve his or her rights to sexual expression when that person is confined to a nursing home, we might have to answer as we would want someone to reply on our own behalf, were we to find ourselves in the same situation. We have to remember that these are human beings that have the same emotional needs we all have. We have to figure out how to meet them in the right settings, with dignity and respect to all the parties involved.

Taking Care of the Caregiver

Put On Your Own Oxygen Mask First

Caregivers face emotional challenges.

Sometimes I just felt like screaming—other times sobbing. The emotional challenges caregivers often face and how they might best be met is an extremely important issue, because if left unaddressed, emotional burnout on the part of the caregiver can lead to serious disintegration of the family and, in some cases, even to incidents of elder abuse.

Resentment

What are some of the things caregivers resent most? Frequently mentioned are such issues as lack of personal time, lack of sleep on a regular basis, lack of respite options, lack of help from the community, and less-than-equal caregiving participation from other members of the family. Other issues, leading to resentment on the part of caregivers include having to give up income-producing work in order to fulfill care-giving responsibilities and frustration at having to deal with complicated insurance and medical forms.

Impatience

For many caregivers, the ability to remain patient and maintain their own emotional equilibrium decreases as the loved one with Alzheimer's disease, or another dementia, slides further down the scale in his or her ability to remember, communicate, or control his or her emotional outbursts and/or bodily functions. Without positive interactions with people other than the one suffering from dementia, the Alzheimer's caregiver can find him- or herself severely compromised by mental exhaustion.

Depression

Depression is very common among Alzheimer's caregivers. Symptoms of depression include but are not limited to lethargy, apathy, frequent crying spells, social withdrawal and isolation, irritability, insomnia or oversleeping, overeating or loss of appetite, lack of libido and in extreme cases, thoughts of suicide. Without ongoing professional support from a social worker, psychotherapist, and/or psychiatrist, as well as options for support group counseling, the situation for the caregiver often gets worse as the disease progresses. And when the one with Alzheimer's approaches the end stages of the disease, it is especially important that the caregiver be given access to hospice-care intervention, bereavement counseling, and spiritual support, if desired.

Other issues for you to explore include

- Feelings of helplessness and hopelessness
- Control issues—sharing control and relinquishing control
- Hypervigilance
- Grief
- Financial challenges

In addition to the common financial and fiscal challenges faced by many Alzheimer caregivers—such as managing finances, managing medical expenses, supervising paid help, and arranging for institutional care when necessitated—there are also increased financial challenges for caregivers who are members of the so-called sandwich generation—that is, those who find themselves in mid-life faced with the dual tasks of rearing young children and caring for elderly parents at the same time. If, in addition to primary caregiving responsibilities, that person is also the main breadwinner of the household or is trying to hold down a job to stay afloat financially, the challenges can feel overwhelming. As if such challenges weren't daunting enough in and of themselves, when Alzheimer's disease becomes a factor in the equation, they become even more greatly magnified.

Yet, as common sense dictates, it is only when we know the true situation that we can begin to change it. So, for a moment, then, let's take a look at some startling, eye-opening, and perhaps altogether sobering statistics that should shine a light on the current situation that exists in America today, regarding the multiple stressors faced by Alzheimer's caregivers, especially those who are trying to balance other competing priorities, such as holding down a job.

According to the Shriver Report (*Alzheimer's in America: The Shriver Report on Women and Alzheimer's—A Study*, by Marie Shriver and the Alzheimer's Association, caregiving falls largely to those who must combine work in the paid labor force with being unpaid caregivers of family members. Sixty percent of all Alzheimer caregivers are women—6.7 million women. Of these women, 56 percent are working. The impact of providing care to a family member with Alzheimer's disease, or other dementias, causes severe strain on their ability to work effectively.

Given the prediction that the demographics are changing drastically in this country—with the aging boomer generation entering retirement in vast numbers, while the combined younger generations (Gen X, Gen Y, and Millennials) are growing at a much lower rate—the scenario takes on an urgent note. A few other pertinent statistics from the report may serve to underline the need to recognize some significant problems encountered by caregivers who have no choice but to remain in the work force:

- "More than 60 percent of working caregivers of people with Alzheimer's reported the need to come in late, leave early or take time off as a result of their caregiving responsibilities."
- "The Alzheimer's Association's Women and Alzheimer's poll reported that more than one-third (34 percent) of women

caregivers of people with Alzheimer's had to give up their job."

Additionally, according to a study by the Families and Work Institute, over the next five years, nearly half of all workers are expecting to be providing family care for an elder. Since the longevity and unpredictability of Alzheimer's disease put a greater burden on working caregivers, for the time and financial resources necessary to fully support their family members, the implications of these findings—especially for those who are taking care of people with Alzheimer's disease—are nothing less than astounding. Some companies have workplace policies that help Alzheimer caregivers remain in the work force, while also fulfilling their caregiving responsibilities. You should explore this with the human resources counselor.

The Family and Medical Leave Act (FMLA) allows those covered by this federal legislation to take up to twelve weeks of unpaid leave per year, which can be taken through reduced schedules or intermittent leave, to care for a spouse or parent with Alzheimer's disease.

It falls short in providing for working caregivers of family members with Alzheimer's. Forty percent of Alzheimer's caregivers are providing care to a relative not covered under the Family and Medical Leave Act. Why? Because the definition of "family" is limited to care for children, parents, and spouses. This means that a worker cannot take leave to care for a parent-in-law, a grandparent, or another relative with Alzheimer's disease. Relatives who fall outside of the FMLA definition of "family" include grandparents, siblings, in-laws, aunt and uncles.

Another way the FMLA law falls short is that it only covers about half of all workers in the United States, due to eligibility requirements for workers and size requirements for employers. Because FMLA does not cover all caregivers, many are at the mercy of their employers when they need to take leave from work to provide care.

Moreover, FMLA allows employers to require their workers to substitute accrued vacation leave, personal leave, or family leave for FMLA leave. As a result, some working caregivers have no time left for themselves or even sick days. Finally, since FMLA leave is unpaid leave, it leaves caregivers with an undue financial burden if they have to miss work or reduce their hours to provide long-term care for an ailing relative with Alzheimer's.

Only two states—New Jersey and California—provide wage replacement for family leave. And this situation persists, despite the fact that the majority of working Alzheimer's caregivers are the primary breadwinners of their household.

In addition to lost wages, women, especially mothers who have already taken time off to raise young children and single women who have never been married or who have not been married long enough—ten years—to qualify for benefits under a spouse's credits, lose the ability to earn credits to qualify for Social Security, when they take time off to provide care for a relative with Alzheimer's.

In order to retain key employees and foster long-term corporate loyalty, a few companies offer such caregiver accommodations as time off, flexible scheduling, and a geriatric care manager. Unfortunately, in today's corporate world, these policies are the exception rather than the rule.

Taking Care of the Caregiver: Difficult and Important Decisions to Be Addressed in Advance

For Patients, Caregivers, and Families: Choosing Care Options for End-Stage Alzheimer's

End of life decisions are difficult and important. Compared with other ultimately fatal conditions, such as terminal cancer and congestive heart failure, Alzheimer's has a long trajectory: from preclinical development and symptomatic onset to ultimate demise, the arc of disease progression can span up to twenty years. By then, everyone involved—including, most of all, the primary caregiver—is either completely exhausted or on the cusp of total collapse and is emotionally spent.

The Importance of Advance Directives

It is best to determine your loved one's wishes for end-stage treatment well ahead of time and preferably early on, when the person is still competent to make informed choices and designate his or her own health care proxies. Basic legal issues related to obtaining such proxies and advance directives have already been addressed in previous chapters. Some people who are still in their right mind have decided that they don't want to be kept alive under any circumstances should they develop dementia.

Controversial End-of-Life Strategy: Voluntarily Stopping Eating and Drinking (VSED)

Startling remarks like these from perfectly coherent people bring up a complex legal scenario hardly noticed much less addressed until recently. Until now, the practice of voluntarily stopping eating and drinking (VSED) was a strategy used by a handful of older people to hasten their decline from terminal conditions, but it was rarely invoked as an end-of-life advance directive. However, with the steep rise of dementia rates in the aging population over the past decades and the projected numbers of those around the world who will eventually be affected by Alzheimer's disease during the middle of the twenty-first century, ethicists, lawyers, and older adults themselves have begun a quiet debate about whether people who develop dementia can use VSED to end their lives by including such instructions in an advance directive.

If VSED is valid for people who are mentally competent, is it also valid for people with dementia? In asking this question, we must infer that, from a legal standpoint, dementia itself is the problem. As the article goes on to explain, the presence of dementia can in fact change a person's eligibility for enforcement of their advance directive with regards to VSED.

Dementia, though a terminal diagnosis, presents unique obstacles for those who want some control over the way they die. Even in the few states where physicians can legally prescribe lethal medication for the terminally ill, laws require that patients be mentally competent and able to ingest those drugs themselves. But demented patients don't qualify for so-called death with dignity. VSED is a lawful way to hasten death for competent adults who find life with a progressive, irreversible disease unendurable. The question for proponents of VSED by advance directive is whether the practice can also provide a humane exit for those who, years later, no longer remember or understand why they wanted to use it.

While the legal status of VSED by advance directive remains virtually untested, the ethical and moral implications of its practice are even more bewildering. The questions below represent the range of valid concerns enmeshed in contemporary legal, moral, and ethical thinking on this issue:

- Can one's current, competent self, make decisions on behalf of one's future demented self?
- Should we encourage people to think their life has no meaning or value because they're in a fragile, vulnerable, and terrible situation?
- Is preemptive suicide by VSED too little, too late?

Far from being definitive, such questions are only the tip of the iceberg in a growing debate of our time.

Transitioning Care Priorities

Yet the real test of end-of-life treatment choices comes when the inevitable reality is staring us in the face from the foot of a hospital bed, whether in a medical facility or a home hospice situation. The decision to transition from lifesaving efforts to comfort care is among the most difficult decisions in life. For families and caregivers—and even for someone with early-stage Alzheimer's—it is therefore best for a person to choose end-of-life preferences beforehand while emotions are still manageable, lest under duress others make a wrongful choice by default.

Although this section deals with choosing treatment options for patients with end-stage Alzheimer's, it has been included in "Taking Care of the Caregiver" because not only do these choices affect the patient's level of comfort and way of passing from this life, but they may also exert a lasting impact on the well-being of the primary caregiver and the entire family. For instance, if you as a caregiver and/or family member are struggling with decisions as to whether or not to initiate life-prolonging interventions or withdraw life support from your loved one, it is important to feel that you have done everything possible not only to act in accordance with advanced directives, but also to avoid interpersonal strife and private feelings of guilt or remorse.

When faced with these life-or-death choices, we must try to proceed in a manner that will mitigate possible family conflict and, at the same time, resolve any future doubts on our own part. The Society of Critical Care Medicine, whose website is quoted below, believes that caregivers and families of end-stage dementia patients are not only compelled to grapple with issues of momentous import but also expected to make these decisions under great duress:

> The decision to transition from life-saving efforts to comfort care is among the most difficult decisions in life. Usually the patient is unable to participate in the decision-making process, leaving the agonizing decisions to family members and loved ones. . . . Knowing that you have honored the patient's beliefs and have acted based on them will help provide comfort. . . . It is important for all of us that we feel we have done everything we can for those afflicted when they are facing death. . . . In many cultures the responsibility for decisions rests with the medical team. This is an acceptable alternative for anyone facing these difficult decisions. Allowing the medical team to make decisions with input from the family may be the most compassionate and appropriate approach.

Important Caveat for Caregivers

Before continuing this discussion any further, however, I want to point out one very important caveat that everyone faced with such a decision should keep in mind: if your loved one does not have a health proxy or a signed advance directive and is in a hospital or other institutional setting, the medical team—

depending on the policy of that facility—may have no choice but to prolong life as long as possible with artificial measures. In many cases, and especially with end-stage Alzheimer's and other dementias, such measures may cause more harm than good.

In these circumstances, the decision to initiate or discontinue life-prolonging interventions may be virtually impossible for a patient's caregiver, health proxy, or family to reverse. Removal of ventilators and feeding tubes can be especially problematic when institutional policy overrides family wishes or caregiver entreaties. Moreover, the emotional and spiritual ramifications of life support withdrawal may haunt the well-intentioned caregiver and possibly ignite polarization and strife in the family.

Arguments Regarding Available Life Support Choices

Bearing in mind the enduring legal and personal reverberations of the Karen Ann Quinlan and Terri Schiavo cases, let us now investigate the variety of life support choices available, explore some common end-stage Alzheimer's care options, and examine the changing definition of "death" in today's complex medical context. In trying to cope with difficult end-of-life decisions, caregivers may benefit from having a few guidelines to rely upon. In this respect, I quote again from the Society of Critical Care Medicine, whose website describes what life support measures can do and gives some parameters for choosing (or not choosing) certain options:

- Life support replaces or supports a failing bodily function. In treatable or curable conditions, life support is used temporarily until the body can resume normal functioning. But, in situations where a cure is not possible, life support may prolong discomfort. , , ,

- A treatment may be helpful if it relieves discomfort, restores functioning, or enhances the quality of life. The same treatment can be considered harmful if it causes pain or

- prolongs the dying process without offering benefit. The outcome may diminish a person's quality of life.
- The decision to refuse life support is a personal one. It is important to talk to your physician regarding the risks and benefits of each therapy. All life support measures are optional treatments.

Top Priority of End-Stage Care: Preventing Suffering

During the end stages of Alzheimer's disease, the top priority becomes to prevent the one from suffering or at least reduce the level of his or her discomfort. When you and your medical team are considering what treatment options to bring to bear, you will need to become familiar with some of the common forms of life support, as well as palliative care and hospice services offered to patients either at home or in nursing homes and medical facilities. Some of these options are listed below for your reference, and many of the definitions used here are directly quoted from the Society of Critical Care Medicine's website, unless otherwise noted.

Comparison of End-Stage Palliative Care and Hospice Care

In this next section, I will compare palliative care and hospice care and discuss the differences between these two very important aspects of end-of-life care. For caregivers, the distinctions between the two protocols mark a critical transition in priorities for the patient. While palliative care and hospice care may overlap in some ways, it is essential to know the difference when you as a dementia caregiver and or family member are faced with these difficult decisions yourself.

Definition of Palliative Care

> Palliative care focuses on reducing the severity of disease symptoms, with the ultimate goal of relieving discomfort and improving the quality of life for patients with serious

illnesses. This care is often provided by a consulting group of clinicians, which may include physicians, nurses, social workers, psychologists, chaplains, and physical, occupational, and other therapists. Palliative care is not the same as hospice care. Patients receiving palliative care have no restrictions on other forms of medical therapy, including life support. Most patients in the ICU have severe illness and benefit from palliative care.

Definition of Hospice Care

Pain and discomfort associated with terminal illness can always be treated.

Comfort Care or Hospice Care?
Comfort care focuses on treating the symptoms of illness when cure is not possible and involves the physical, psychological, and spiritual needs of the patient. The goal is to achieve the best quality of life available by relieving discomfort, controlling pain, and achieving maximum independence. Respect for the patient's culture, beliefs, and values is an essential component of this care.

Hospice is a type of comfort care given by a dedicated team of clinicians either in an inpatient institution or at the patient's home.

In support of our quest to better differentiate between hospice care and palliative care, the quotations below have been excerpted from *What Your Doctor Won't Tell You About Getting Older* by Dr. Lachs:

> Used liberally, the words hospice or hospice care generally refer to a philosophy of care rendered to people with limited life expectancy. It, too, focuses on symptom relief and providing comfort to patients and families during those difficult times; hospice care also philosophically accepts the dying process as a natural part of life. Accordingly, much of

7. Taking Care of the Caregiver

the work of hospice involves palliative care but for patients with a limited prognosis.

Cessation of Medical Treatment: A Key Aspect of Hospice

It is imperative for us to note one key aspect of hospice that many people fail to realize- namely, that for patients entering hospice care, all medical treatment other than pain relief ceases. In practice, this means no hydration, no blood transfusions, for example, as normally these interventions are not part of hospice protocol.

In the United States, hospice care can have an even more specific meaning: It refers to a Part A Medicare benefit to which beneficiaries are entitled (most private insurers have adopted similar policies and benefits). And just as palliative care isn't only for cancer patients, you need not have cancer to be enrolled in a hospice program. In fact, hospice is underused for many clinical conditions, including Alzheimer's and other illnesses.

Hospice care can be delivered in many places: at a hospice site, at home, in nursing homes, and sometimes in the hospital. Hospice patients are always followed by a physician; in some cases this is a physician who works for the hospice, but many physicians (and especially geriatricians) follow their patients into hospice. In order for someone to be enrolled, a physician must certify that the patient has a prognosis of less than six months (sounds ironclad, but fret not; it rarely is— many patients in hospice outlive their six-month certification, in which case they can be recertified or even taken off hospice if their condition or prognosis improves). Enrollment brings a variety of services to the patient that would not normally be covered by Medicare: visiting nurses, social workers, family support, and so on. In general, patients who choose the Medicare hospice benefit forgo subsequent hospitalization, although if circumstances warrant, such as a hip fracture, this can be overridden.

Timing Critical in Ensuring Adequate Pain Relief

As caregivers and families proceed further down the path which at this point the one with advanced dementia is irreversibly on, a timely question to consider is when to call for palliative care. Some common errors in how palliative care is delivered occur repeatedly throughout the United States. The most common: Consultation is requested too late. Suffering that has been ongoing could have been treated days sooner. What can you do to avoid this problem? . . . Nurses and social workers can determine when palliative care is reasonable. The Visiting Nurse Service may also be of assistance at this time.

Important Role of a Compassionate Medical Team

When palliative and hospice care are administered by a compassionate medical team, caregivers and families can rest assured that they have done everything possible to keep their departing ones as comfortable as possible during their transition from this life to the next. This assurance can go a long way in helping caregivers and families avoid feelings of guilt when their loved one experiences a painless and peaceful demise. Families still have an important role to play in maintaining a sense of the patient's self, even when that person's selfhood is no longer in residence.

Common Euphemisms for Death

The reality of death and dying makes us uneasy, so we use euphemisms to indirectly reference death. Attempts to avoid confronting this are typical in our society. Many find that even saying the word "death" is difficult.

To this end, there are more than one hundred euphemisms for death in the English language alone. For instance, a person who has died is said to have "crossed over," "given up the ghost," "fallen asleep," "met his maker," "passed on," "passed away," "gone to his/her just reward," or "shuffled off this mortal coil" (to use Shakespeare's lines from *Hamlet*). Other less serious or even irreverent euphemisms for "death" include such colloquialisms as "cashed in his chips," "bit the dust," "walked the plank," "flatlined," "croaked," or "kicked the bucket." But regardless of how a person chooses to hide or express his or her concept of death, the truth remains: Death is still one reality none of us can ultimately avoid.

Giving Up Caregiving

Death is the final phase of dementia caregiving, and it is not surprising that many caregivers find this phase the most difficult. This is perhaps because it involves the painful task of letting go of our loved ones and everything about them that we have been clinging to for so long. Yet, as if this task alone were not enough to put a whole family into crisis mode, what is now considered "death" has become infinitely more complex—partly because of the recent advances made in life support technologies.

Eight Indicators That Death Is Imminent

Common observations that death is near are.:

1. Inability to close the eyelids

2. Diminishing ability to react to visual stimulation

3. A reduced ability to react to sounds and words

4. Facial drooping

5. Nonreactive pupils

6. Hyperextension of the neck (This causes the head to tilt farther back when lying down.)

7. Vocal cord grunting

8. Bleeding in the upper digestive tract

Definition of "Life Support"

"Life support" refers to a spectrum of techniques, used to maintain life after the failure of one or more vital organs.

Life Support Choices

Mechanical Ventilation (MV)
Mechanical ventilation is used to support or replace the function of the lungs. A machine called a ventilator (or respirator) forces air into the lungs through a tube inserted into the mouth (or rarely into the nose or neck) and down into the windpipe (trachea). This breathing support may be used for a short time (for example, treating pneumonia), or it may be needed indefinitely for permanent lung disease or trauma to the brain. Some patients on long-term MV live a quality of life that is acceptable to them. For other patients, MV may only prolong the dying process.

Artificial Nutrition and Hydration
Liquid nutrition and hydrating fluids may be given into the gut (tube feeding) or directly into the bloodstream (intravenous feeding) until the patient can eat and drink again. Although potentially valuable and lifesaving in some situations, artificial nutrition and hydration do not make dying patients more comfortable. Scientific evidence shows that patients can die comfortably without artificial nutrition or hydration.

7. Taking Care of the Caregiver

Intravenous Hydration

Intravenous (IV) rehydration is used for moderate to severe cases of dehydration. The treatment involves a steady injection of fluid including water and dissolved salts (electrolytes) into a vein. The kind of fluid used depends on the situation, but it usually consists of water with a little salt or sugar added.

Tube Feeding

Tube feeding gives a chemically balanced mix of nutrients and fluids through a feeding tube. Most commonly, this tube is inserted into the stomach through the nose or through the wall of the abdomen by means of a surgical procedure. Another type of feeding tube is inserted surgically through the abdominal wall into the small intestine.

IV Feeding (parenteral nutrition)

IV feedings are given to patients who are unable to receive tube feedings. As with tube feedings, the IV feeding provides the patient with the needed amount of protein, carbohydrate, fat, vitamins, and minerals.

Do Not Resuscitate

A Do Not Resuscitate (DNR) Order is also known as a Do Not Attempt Resuscitation (DNAR) Order. If you or not wish to receive cardiopulmonary resuscitation (CPR) your physician must write a DNAR order in the chart. This order can be changed at any time for any reason.

Issues of Informed Consent of Prime Concern

From our earlier examination of the use of VSED, or voluntarily stopping eating and drinking and the removal of other life support interventions for patients at the end stage of Alzheimer's disease and other dementias, we have seen that issues surrounding the idea of informed consent are of prime concern. As we consider all of the end-of-life care options available to families and caregivers, it is my sincere hope that raising these often controversial issues will give you a stronger foundation upon which to base your decisions in the best interest of the loved one, as he or she passes from this life into the great beyond.

Some Food for Thought

On a final note, as we come to the end of this sad but necessary chapter, I would like to leave you with a few uplifting thoughts for your consideration.

Taking Care of the Caregiver: Accepting the Inevitable

Coping with Final Decline and Death and Building Bridges to New Hope
Having to say goodbye to a beloved person is never easy. But with Alzheimer's disease, it is even more difficult. It has already been a long, hard journey—sometimes more than seven years—from onset to end stage. With Alzheimer's, the arrival of death is slow, but relentless. For the family—and especially for the caregiver—there is frequently a sense of overwhelming exhaustion, perhaps tinged with regret, remorse, guilt, and, more often than not, relief.

For those of us who, as Alzheimer's caregivers, have walked the long walk with our loved one, gently guiding the way past untold obstacles and trying to maintain a modicum of normalcy in an increasingly distorted and surreal landscape, the last lap of the journey can represent two sides of a coin. One side is the loss of one's own identity (especially on the part of the primary caregiver). The other side is release from an almost impossible burden.

How this conflict plays out in each individual and family is a matter of great variance, albeit, with similar themes and common emotional reactions. Because of the intensity of our feelings at this watershed point in life, it is all the more important for caregivers and family members alike to avail themselves of all the practical and spiritual support they can get. The Alzheimer's Association has a twenty-four-hour hot-line (1-800-272-3900) and many support groups to help soon-to-be-bereaved people cope with their impending loss.

As we approach the inevitable "Valley of the Shadow" on the arduous journey through Alzheimer's, we need to know what to expect when our loved one is nearing the finish line. We need to know what our options are when it comes to arranging for hospice care and learning how to let go, even though we held on so tightly before in an effort to keep our ailing loved one safe and out of danger.

7. Taking Care of the Caregiver

Not everyone suffering with end-stage Alzheimer's disease has the option to choose euthanasia as an advanced directive. Euthanasia is illegal in the United States. Some states, such as Washington, Oregon, Montana, and Vermont, do allow for physician-assisted suicide, in which doctors provide terminally ill patients with the means to end their own life. Physician-assisted suicide is not available for nonterminally ill patients.

Even though Alzheimer's disease is indeed terminal (that is, ultimately fatal), for most people suffering with this disease in the United States, neither euthanasia nor physician-assisted suicide is an option. Rather, the end of life is spent in an institutional hospice setting, or in a hospice-like situation at home. This is the period when hard decisions are faced by families, having to do with the insertion of feeding tubes and the vigor with which medical measures should be taken to fend off those natural processes that descend like jackals—or perhaps like friends—on debilitated people.

And family members, who at this point have been bombarded with conflicting emotions and are perhaps struggling with contradictory value systems, have to accept the consequences of those hard decisions.

The difficulty of deciding is compounded by the difficulty of living with what has been decided. If it is decided not to tube-feed, death by starvation may be a merciful choice for people who are unconscious or otherwise without sensation of the process. Starvation may well seem preferable to the alternatives, the paralysis and the malnutrition that almost inevitably overtake even the most scrupulously fed of intubated terminally ill people. The great majority of people in an Alzheimer's vegetative state will die of some sort of infection.

As bodily functions close down, one by one, a person gradually loses consciousness and passes from this life. In a typical hospice situation, when the end is near, the patient's mouth is kept moistened, but food and drink are withheld, as the swallowing mechanism has ceased to function and aspiration (choking) is to be avoided. The patient is kept warm and in as comfortable a state as possible. By this time, there is usually little, if any, cognitive function left.

By this time, the family and caretakers of the dying person have been worn down to a frazzle, with the weight of their isolation, exhaustion, and impending grief: It often seems as though the families of Alzheimer's patients are sidetracked from the broad sunlit avenues of ongoing life, remaining trapped for years, each family in its own excruciating cul-de-sac. The only rescue comes with the death of a person they love. And even then, the memories and the dreadful toll drag on, and from these the release can only be partial. A life that has been well lived and a shared sense of happiness and accomplishment are ever after seen through the smudged glass of its last few years. For the survivors, the concourse of existence has forever become less bright and less direct.

Nevertheless, the time of impending bereavement is when people most need the support of friends, counselors, and clergy. Seeking a spiritual perspective can help us build a bridge for ourselves and for our loved one. Following the spiritual practices and traditions of our heritage and honoring the ethical stance and loving deeds of our loved one in his or her better days can help us preserve important memories and legacies. Perhaps, through reliving special times together, you may be able to discover a way to clear some of the darkness from that "smudged glass" and bring back to mind the joyful light of that person whom you loved so dearly and are now losing.

Some people find it helpful to start this process long before the person suffering from dementia loses the ability to remember and communicate those memories. Making tape recordings of friends and family members talking about their good times together and about their challenges in life can be helpful in passing along important values. Photo albums and videos can also be helpful in preserving the legacy of shared experience. Playing music, singing, reading poetry, and displaying hand-made items and artwork can also serve to illuminate the loving spirit, competence, and/or sense of humor of the person whom we love.

Throughout history and in diverse cultures, ritual has been instrumental in helping people cope with the unknown, the unexplained, and the irreparably lost. Bereaved people may find a profound sense of comfort and solace in their religious heritage and practice. Some may experience emotional healing in the process of planning a memorial tribute to their loved one. Others may discover meaning in contributing to worthy causes or setting up legacy funds to support ongoing work in a field in which their loved one was once involved.

In addition, many charitable organizations—such as Mothers Against Drunk Driving—have grown out of the desire of a bereaved family to do something about a situation that caused their loved one's death. HousingWorks is another example, a nonprofit organization that was founded in response to the thousands of AIDS deaths in America over the past three decades. This group, which operates high-end thrift shops to help people living with HIV and AIDS avoid poverty, isolation, and homelessness, has been recognized for having developed an outstanding not-for-profit business model. And there are many Alzheimer's-related organizations—such as the Alzheimer's Association–that were founded to help dementia patients and their caregivers and families cope with the challenges posed by neuro-degenerative diseases. So, whatever direction our hearts choose to lead us, somehow or other—even in the midst of our utter exhaustion and darkest despair—we must begin searching for ways to build a bridge from where we are now as the final curtain comes down to where we might be when the lights come up again.

After an initial period of intense mourning and additional months of extended recovery, many bereaved families and caregivers decide to offer their own experience in support of others who are serving as Alzheimer's or dementia caregivers. How you express your wish to honor your loved one is an individual matter. Some people may need to relive old memories and mourn in private. Others may prefer a more active involvement. But, whatever your mode of expression, it is important to give yourself some credit for who you are and what you have done, even as you mourn the loss of your loved one.

A gradual approach to reengagement with the world can be beneficial to a caregiver who has felt isolated and trapped in the caregiving world. It is not necessary to wave flags or volunteer for a flurry of activities while you are still in the shadow of impending or recent death. What is important is to pay attention to your own needs, as you tended to the needs of your loved one. When you are able, to reenter the so-called "real" world, you will find your own path back to normalcy. Meanwhile, do allow some time for reflection and reconnection with supportive people before you venture out into the larger community. In grappling with grief, time is your ally. At this point, getting enough sleep, eating properly, and allowing others to be there for you are part of the healing process. You will reemerge when you are ready.

After a while, as you begin to heal, you may experience a sense of boredom. Or you may feel the urge to get more involved with your friends, return to work, or become more active in your community. You may also start to see opportunities for service with an advocacy group such as the Alzheimer's Association, which has chapters all around the country. You may want to try your hand at becoming active in a local context. As you continue to heal, you may see more possibilities for even greater service.

Several high-profile celebrities whose lives have been deeply touched by Alzheimer's have made an indelible impact on public awareness of this devastating disease. And some (perhaps not-so-famous) Alzheimer's survivors have worked tirelessly to create a great public legacy from their caregiving experiences. Of the more notable Alzheimer's survivors in the first category, two people come to mind for their singular contributions to Alzheimer's-related activism. Princess Yasmin Aga Khan, whose mother, Rita Hayworth, suffered from Alzheimer's, has, become a great advocate for Alzheimer's Association initiatives and a stellar fundraiser for its efforts to underwrite Alzheimer's research and provide caregiver support around the clock. And award-winning journalist Maria Shriver, whose father, Sargent Shriver, was one of the most prominent government officials to succumb to Alzheimer's, has collaborated with the Alzheimer's Association by authoring two groundbreaking reports describing Alzheimer's current and future impact on American society in general and on women, in particular. Both of these women lost a beloved parent to Alzheimer's. And both of these inspiring women exemplify what far-reaching effects one person can have when motivated by an overarching desire to serve a goal much greater than oneself.

Other bereaved caregivers have written books, presented plays, or produced films and documentaries, some of which have garnered national attention and critical acclaim. Because of their efforts, and the efforts of countless other caregivers as well as researchers, clinicians, and advocates, the reality of Alzheimer's has now emerged from the shadows into the limelight. Millions of people around the world are finally starting to realize that we are all impacted by this disease in one way or another.

We each have to find our own way over time to fill the hole in our soul that this personal loss and ordeal leaves us with. Solitude was my comfort for many months.

Meditation

Meditation was a way of life for me as a Quaker. It is widely accepted today for many situations: from pain relief and stress reduction to finding inner peace. Most medical centers offer classes in how to meditate, as well as many private organizations and individuals. Corporate America has recognized the benefits of having calm employees. As a result, many companies offer classes and on-site spaces to learn and practice meditation. For caregivers, it is a meaningful relief to be able to relax and clear one's mind for a few moments or more. The science is indisputable.

The Shamatha Project, conducted at the University of California–Davis and San Francisco, is the most comprehensive longitudinal study of intensive meditation. The research team measured telomerase activity in participants who had completed a three-month intensive meditation retreat.

Positive psychological changes that occur during meditation training are associated with greater telomerase activity, according to researchers, The study is the first to link positive well-being to higher telomerase, an enzyme important for the long-term health of cells in the body. The effect appears to be attributable to psychological changes that increase a person's ability to cope with stress and maintain feelings of well-being.

Meditation is known to promote positive psychological changes.

The take-home message is that high telomerase activity was due to the beneficial effects of meditation on perceived control and neuroticism, which in turn, were due to changes in mindfulness and sense of purpose.

Caregiver, Who Are You?: Identity Crisis

Spouse, Friend, Lover, or Stranger?
Caring for someone with Alzheimer's disease, on an ongoing basis, can have many side effects that prey on the body and soul. Especially troublesome are the aches, pains, and heartache created by stress and fatigue. But perhaps the worst side effect of all for the devoted caregiver is knowing that whatever you are doing is not going to restore health to your loved one but will only help ease their downward spiral to increased isolation, then to solitary existence, and ultimately to death. And, to add insult to injury, the realization that you will eventually become strangers to one another in spite of your previous relationship is a heavy burden for any caregiver to endure, especially as the situation continues to change over the course of time. One day, you are recognized by your loved one, and the next you are a complete stranger—one who may be either welcomed or feared. The length that the course of the disease takes offers no relief and often intensifies as the other factors accompanying the disease kick-in: health, financial, family, and the unknown.

On the one hand, to the mentally challenged person with Alzheimer's whose own sense of self is fast slipping away, the increasing sense of uncertainty of who you, the caregiver, are, can be totally devastating. From the perspective of someone suffering from Alzheimer's, the role of his or her caregiver changes as the disease progresses: first, you are a helping hand and a welcome companion; next, you are just the person who helps with bathing, dressing, and keeping an eye on things; then you are the one who tries to get him or her to be social, to eat, and to exercise. Finally, the day comes when your loved one can no longer remember exactly who you are: Are you the wife, a friend, or someone else? Who are you?

I found as a caregiver, every fiber of my being was challenged and maybe discarded by my husband who now, thanks to Alzheimer's, had no memory of who I had been to him not so very long before. Moreover, this de facto rejection (albeit unavoidable and no fault of the loved one) can cause feelings of significant identity loss on the part of the caregiver. For example, if you had previously defined yourself as someone's loving wife or husband and equal partner in life, you may wonder who you are now that you've had to become the one in charge while your partner can hardly be there with you, much less for you. Moreover, trying to maintain a sexual relationship with someone who may or may not recognize you is disconcerting, to say the least! As a person trying to balance the dual roles of caregiver and spouse, one must understand that in the early and middle stages of Alzheimer's disease, sexual desire is still a compelling factor, and each person must relate according to his or her own history. This is not easy, as turning your mind and passion from caregiving to being a lover poses a strong challenge for anyone in this situation.

Another part of the havoc brought on by Alzheimer's disease is the onset of disturbing personality changes that often come about as the dementia progresses. Traits that are entirely new to you may surface unexpectedly and these traits are not usually endearing ones! In my case, Bill could be very rude and became extremely jealous of my conversations with other people. Toward the end of his life things got even worse. One time, when I was trying to get him to eat, he spat the food at me, blurting out, "This is what I think of you!" Yet, during the beginning and middle stages of Alzheimer's disease, Bill was his usual loving and tender self who did not want me to leave him with other people. He would call me multiple times when I was at work just to reassure himself. So here I want to point out that, as compassionate caregivers, we should try to remember what a very frightening and frustrating experience it must be for those who suffer from this ravaging disease to lose the sense of who they are and what is happening to them.

When Alzheimer's disease strikes one member of a family, unknown (or at least heretofore unexpressed) character traits in other family members have a way of rearing their ugly heads, often without warning. This happened to us, as well. The times when I had to travel for business were always very difficult. The symptoms that were perplexing in 1995 were confirmed in October 1996 as

Alzheimer's. This was the beginning of a very difficult period of for both me and Bill, lasting five years, until his death.

The business trips I had to make to Japan and China usually lasted ten days and were quite scary for Bill as well as for me. Bill would call me long distance with pleas to come home. I would become so stressed out that I often developed severe muscle spasms to the point where I was absolutely exhausted but could not sleep. On one long transcontinental flight, I was worried sick, in considerable pain and generally miserable. But, fortunately for me, the flight attendants were very helpful with handing out mineral ice, as they were well accustomed to dealing with stressed-out international business travelers.

I think one of the most important things for a caregiver to keep in mind is that prolonged stress itself can cause painful reactions in the body that may differ from one individual to another. One person may develop migraine headaches or chest pains; another might suffer from severe muscle spasms, as I did; and someone else could experience asthma attacks or episodes of painful sciatica. The list goes on. But since Alzheimer's disease usually lasts for a long period, over time these maladies can add up and, when compounded, possibly disable the caregiver if left untreated, thus placing the loved one in an even more vulnerable position. So, when the stress begins to mount up, it is imperative that Alzheimer caregivers seek relief from their ongoing physical symptoms as soon as possible and without guilt.

Yet, despite our own personal aches and pains, we as caregivers must not lose sight of the whole picture. While there are obviously ways to mitigate some of the somatic distress that many primary caregivers are subject to, the emotional toll of Alzheimer's disease on caregivers may not be so readily apparent or as easily remediable. Nevertheless, the emotional toll is certainly just as significant as the physical toll, if not more so. We are not alone. Millions are experiencing our anxiety and problems.

In 2018, The Alzheimer's Association reported that 16 million caregivers gave 18.4 billion hours of unpaid home care, valued at more than $232 billion.

After Bill's failed stent operation, Bill became the person that many caregivers eventually face in a home situation—unable to perform any self-care, incontinent, experiencing loss of bowel control, unable to feed himself, and often confined to bed. Caring for a person in this condition is like caring for a baby, but this baby is an adult and often combative. Diaper changes are difficult with adults, changes of linens are often necessary, and the physical demands this presents are enormous and impossible to handle alone. In many instances, both people are adults and frail and this adds to an already-taxing situation. Help is not always available for a task that needs twenty-four-hour care. Anxiety on the part of both people, although it may be expressed differently, adds to the ongoing wear and tear.

When Bill was at home for the first five years after the onset of the disease and before the stent operation, I was constantly listening to him sleeping, waiting for his call, and alert that he might be awake and walking around. How do you half-sleep? You are always tired. Even in our situation, with other people in the home, it was my watch. I did not have to do the physical house care that many others do, but I realize the toll it must be to have that additional burden.

Lack of physical exercise for both people presents health issues. Exercise is necessary—both physically and mentally—to keep one's balance in life. Inactivity leads to a loss of bone calcium and to skeletal issues. Physical activity is needed for brain health.

The constant watching of each other for different reasons is not a healthy state of mind. The years mounted. I became an anxious person, inwardly, always waiting for the next hurdle. Would it be Bill, his children, or something else? We were lucky with stable, reliable caregivers, in-house help, caring friends, and financial resources. For others less fortunate, who need to seek aid from the community, there are resources. The churches and other faith-based organizations often have volunteers who will perform various kinds of tasks, from caregiving and driving to preparing meals. The Alzheimer's Association offers workshops and support groups for caregivers. Your insurance agent or social worker may also be able to provide some alternatives and solutions. But whatever your circumstances, with Alzheimer's, it is a long, tough go.

8

Death

Rediscovering and Recovering Your Self and Picking Up the Pieces of Your Own Life

I don't think there's any way to go through the caregiving experience without coming out on the other side a different person. How you, the caregiver, feel when it's all over depends on many factors: your own temperament and circumstances, the nature of your relationship with the person you have cared for, what kinds of demands were imposed on you, the resources available, and how your loved one's final days unfolded. Other issues include resolving family and money issues, grappling with an altered sense of identity, and processing the entire experience of caregiving.

Grappling with an altered sense of identity can pose a particularly acute problem for caregivers, even before the death of a person with Alzheimer's disease occurs, because the lack of recognition by the loved one usually precedes his or her death by months or even years. If your own spouse or parent (or any other relative) can't remember who you are, you, in a sense, can no longer maintain the same relationship with them (that is, as husband and wife or parent and child) as you had before the dementia set in.

As far as processing the entire experience of caregiving is concerned, this is a task requiring time and a willingness to open up to the myriad implications of one's life in selfless service to the needs of another person. The ramifications of this experience can be surprising and sometimes very painful.

After the death of your loved one, the new question becomes, "Where is my place in the world now?" Finding or creating that new place is the great challenge for the former caregiver. After a necessary, but sometimes prolonged period of physical recovery and personal reflection, many people look for ways to go back to caretaking and become of more service to others. However, returning to a caregiving role may not be the best route for a former caregiver to take immediately after the death of his or her loved one. What must be done first is to reestablish one's own sense of self. Then later, at an appropriate time in the future, one can explore these potential avenues of caring expression, which may include such options as changing one's previous career, volunteering at a local respite program, participating in spiritually enriching activities, becoming an Alzheimer's activist, or setting up a foundation or financial legacy. But before this external reinvention of your life can take place, it is important that you first spend some time getting back in touch with your own true, and most likely unexpressed or deeply submerged, self.

In the Wake of Alzheimer's: A Caregiver's Struggle for Wholeness When Death Occurs

For those of us who have survived the upheaval of Alzheimer's, the safest place to be is in the matrix of our deepest human connections—family members, close friends, care partners, spiritual kinships, and fellow survivors. It is here that we can brace ourselves against the devastation of exhaustion and grief and renew our energies, finding strength in the unseen safety net that connects us all.

What is resilience? It is the ability to bounce back after devastation and catastrophe. We as caregivers have spent our energies on someone we loved. We have trudged up the mountain, carrying the enormous weight of Alzheimer's on our shoulders. Now we must seek the hidden springboard beneath our feet. In the warm embrace of loving friends and fellow travelers, we will seek the strength to reinvent ourselves and carry out our life's continuing purpose. In the warm sunlight we will find a safe place to grow new seeds and forge new connections into the future.

Everyone Has Resilience

New research into resilience has found that our brain's innate neuroplasticity enables us to develop our own unique barrier of "psychological Teflon" to handle life's hurdles and hardships, allowing us to bounce back better from setbacks, adapt better to change, and manage stress more effectively.

Resilience is, therefore, not some either/or trait that only a lucky few are genetically endowed with. Rather it sits on a continuum and wherever you might be sitting on it today, you are never too old, too weak, or too wimpy to strengthen your ability to handle the problems and challenges that may be coming your way tomorrow.

Elevate Your Perspective
By looking at your current problems through a much wider, you can see your problems in a different perspective. Exercising, meditating, gardening, journaling, and listening to or playing music are all activities that not only help keep stress in check but expand your capacity for life's inevitable surprises.

Don't Let Your Situation Define You
As different as the circumstances are after heartache and hardships, you must reclaim your identity to experience the challenges of life. Our heartaches, hurdles, and hardships can shape us, but they don't have to define us. When life deals us particularly tough blows, we have to be even more vigilant about not succumbing to a victim mentality, which can render us powerless to shape our future and respond to our challenges in a way that extracts wisdom form them, increases confidence in ourselves, and adds a deeper dimension to our experience of life.

Accept Reality; Don't Fight It
We need to accept that life will often be difficult, that bad things will happen to good people (including yourself), and that even the best-laid plans will sometimes come unglued through no fault of your own. Accepting reality can

spare you an enormous amount of unnecessary suffering.

Don't waste your energy complaining. Instead, make the most of what you can do with the resources you do have (your intelligence being first among them). Many people spend a lot of time complaining or fretting about what might happen in the future and spend too little time in purposeful action setting themselves up to handle the possibilities that the future may bring.

We know that people who have a stronger support network cope better in difficult times and recover faster from illness than those without one. Oxytocin is our body's own resilience-building hormone—a part of our body's natural stress response in times of crisis.

So even if your inclination is to battle it out on your own, don't. A burden shared, is a burden halved. Don't let false pride, timidity, or reticence to appear needy keep you from reaching out, sharing what you're dealing with, and asking for support. It could literally add years to your life.

Relationship to Post-Traumatic Growth

"Post-traumatic growth" is defined as a positive change, as a result of experiencing a traumatic event. Whereas "resilience" refers to characteristics acquired prior to the traumatic event, post-traumatic growth has been described as going beyond resilience by transforming and building upon the experience to create a positive outlook. This growth process often takes time, during which individuals may report continuing distress following the trauma.

When Your Loved One Is Gone: In the Valley of the Shadow—Facing Death

Death is a subject that has both fascinated and repelled our species since the dawn of time. For millennia, human beings have been in search of a way to delay, avoid, outsmart, or destroy death. The ancient pharaohs tried to defy death by creating pyramids and filling them with artifacts to supply their needs in the afterlife. They also took their spouses, servants, and horses along to keep them company.

Death finally comes. You have to accept it. You have to let go of what you have so desperately held on to for so long. You have no other choice. When one is going through the valley of the shadow of death, it seems as though there is no end to the sadness that surrounds us, the living, like a shroud. But you have been that caring person for your loved one. You have been a blessing for them.

Now you must mourn and bear witness to that life that once lived and laughed but has now left you here, sad and alone. And, somehow, you must find a way to go on, even though the shadow seems to follow.

Dealing with Grief and Bereavement: Taking the Time You Need

One of the great pioneers in grief research was psychiatrist Dr. Elisabeth Kübler-Ross (1926–2004). She was educated at the University of Zurich, taught at the University of Chicago, and practiced medicine in the United States. Author of the landmark book *On Death and Dying* (1969), she called death called the "greatest mystery in science."

Over the course of her prolific career, she opened up a topic that had previously been ignored, not only in public discourse but in medical education as well as. Her work, as a result, revolutionized the treatment of the terminally ill and their families in this country. During her career, Kübler-Ross wrote more than twenty books on death and related subjects, including *To Live Until We Say Goodbye* (1978), *Living with Death and Dying* (1981), and *The Tunnel and the Light* (1999). Her final book, *On Grief and Grieving* (2005), was written with David Kessler. She also traveled around the world, giving her "Life, Death, and Transition" workshops.

According to Dr. Kübler-Ross, there are five stages of grief: denial, anger, bargaining, depression, and acceptance. The identification of these stages was a revolutionary concept at the time but has since become widely accepted. Although these five stages were initially intended to describe a dying person's trajectory through grief, they also can aptly describe the reaction of a devoted caregiver or family member of the dying person. Each of us experiences grief differently. I think it is important to be patient as we go through each stage. to seek professional help when needed, and to accept the fact that both the afflicted and you, as a caregiver, may have the same emotional roller coaster. These are legitimate feelings and the process of grief takes time.

While these stages of the grief cycle express what a dying person often goes through, if they are conscious, Alzheimer's caregivers and other survivors of a loved one's death can also experience similar reactions, although perhaps not in such a lock-step order. In fact, it is common for a person to experience several of these stages at one time. But no matter what stage or stages of grief you find yourself in during a particular time span, the important things to remember are that what you are feeling is legitimate and that processing grief takes time. Throughout the entire grieving process, a bereaved person may take solace in finding within his or her encounters with life and death some purpose or meaning, however you might want to define those concepts.

Perhaps for many, poetry is one helpful way of dealing with grief. Anger and outrage are aspects of grief that we often don't want to admit to feeling. Yet, one does at times want to scream at the injustice of death. One powerful voice to express an overwhelming sense of outrage in the face of death is that of Dylan Thomas. According to one website, Dylan Thomas's most famous poem, known by its first line "Do Not Go Gentle into That Good Night," is also the most famous example of the poetic form known as the villanelle. Yet, the poem's true importance lies not in its fame, but in the raw power of the emotions underlying it. Thomas uses the poem to address his dying father, lamenting his father's loss of health and strength and encouraging him to cling to life. The urgency of the speaker's tone has kept the poem among the world's most-read works in English for more than half a century.

Looking Ahead into the Future: What Is Our Best Hope? Answer: The Human Spirit, Alzheimer's Research, and the Ongoing Search for a Cure

> Hope is the thing with feathers that perches in the soul—and sings the tunes without the words—and never stops at all.
>
> —Emily Dickenson

> He who has health, has hope; and he who has hope, has everything.
>
> —Thomas Carlyle

> While there's life, there's hope.
>
> —Marcus Tullius Cicero

By now, we all are acutely aware of Alzheimer's disease. It is no longer a back-room, hushed-up condition in which the person suffering from dementia has been relegated to a virtual dungeon of disregard and shame and his or her family and caregivers have become the brunt of social stigma and its resultant marginalization. At this point, we Americans are finally starting to realize that our entire society, and the global society of humankind, is under increasing threat daily from this devastating and inexorably destructive disease—one for which causes are not completely understood and cures not even envisioned on the far distant horizon. Yet, despite these vast unknowns, we cannot—indeed must not—give up the search for answers to these overwhelming questions. We cannot stop trying to find more compassionate care and effective treatment for dementia sufferers and more realistic support and respite options for their families and caregivers.

Hope is considered by many to be a mindset of last resort. According to the words of Saint Paul (1 Corinthians 13:13), of the three greatest virtues—faith, hope, and love—hope is not considered the most important. That honor belongs to love, or charity, as it is often translated. Yet when everything else is gone, our faith having been tested to its limit and our love stretched so thin that we can scarcely believe there is anything left but exhaustion, then and only then do we realize the importance and value of hope.

Hope is what remains when every other option is seemingly blocked. Hope is what keeps us going. And hope is what we hold on to when the ground of our existence is trembling beneath our feet and the sky of our dreams is crashing down upon our head.

Hope is what keeps physicians and researchers pushing the boundaries of

8. Death

knowledge and clinical protocols. Hope is what drives fundraising appeals for new initiatives in patient care and family and caregiver support. And it is hope for the next generation that wells up in our hearts when there is nothing more we can do for our ailing loved one.

Yet all too often hope is thought of as an exercise in futility. Why should we continue to hope when there seems to be no reason to? Hope is too flimsy, too ineffectual, and too weak for us to give it much credence. But what is its alternative—to give up and abandon the struggle to find a cure for Alzheimer's and end the terrible suffering it inevitably inflicts upon its victims?

So, we march on and we cling to hope. But we are not alone: thousands walk with us. We have borne a lighted torch, those of us who have been caregivers and family members, advocates and advisors, healers and scholars, and we must pass that torch to those who can carry it further aloft, to enlighten others and underwrite further research and caregiving relatives, even to some who can carry it into the highest halls of government.

Glossary of Alzheimer's Disease Terms

Abilities: The level at which certain actions and activities can be carried out.

Acetylcholine: A chemical in the brain, a neurotransmitter, that appears to be involved in learning and memory. Acetylcholine is greatly diminished in the brains of people with Alzheimer's disease.

Activities of Daily Living (ADL): Activities that are necessary for everyday living and independent functioning, such as eating, bathing, grooming, dressing, and toileting.

Adjuvant Therapy: Treatment provided in addition to the primary treatment.

Adult-Day-Care Services: Programs that provide participants with opportunities to interact with others, usually in a community center or dedicated facility. People come and go from the center on a daily basis.

Advance Directive (Living Will): A document written and signed when in good health, that informs your family and health care providers of your wishes about extended medical treatment in times of emergency.

Adverse Reaction: An unexpected effect of drug treatment that may range from minor to serious to life threatening, such as an allergic reaction.

Aggression: Hitting, pushing, or threatening behavior that may occur when a caregiver tries to help an Alzheimer's patient with daily activities, such as grooming and/or dressing.

Agitation: Behavior such as screaming, shouting, complaining, moaning, cursing, pacing, fidgeting, wandering, and so on that is disruptive, unsafe, or interferes with the delivery of care in a particular environment.

Alternative Therapies: The use of techniques other than drugs, surgery, or other conventional therapies to treat disease and manage long-term pain. Some common alternative therapies, also called complementary therapies, include the use of herbs, meditation, exercise, magnets, reflexology, massage, and acupuncture.

Alzheimer's Disease: A progressive disease in which nerve cells in the brain become damaged and brain matter shrinks, resulting in impaired thinking, behavior, and memory.

Ambulation: The ability to walk and move about freely.

Amyloid: A protein deposit associated with tissue damage and breakdown. Amyloid is found in the brains of individuals with Alzheimer's disease.

Amyloid Plaque: Abnormal clusters of dead and dying nerve cells, other brain cells, and amyloid protein fragments.

Antibodies: Specialized proteins produced by the cells of the immune system that counteract specific foreign substances.

Antidepressants: Medications used to treat depression. Antidepressants are not addictive; they do not make you high or produce a craving for more.

Anti-inflammatory Drugs: Drugs that reduce inflammation or swelling.

Anxiety: A feeling of apprehension, fear, nervousness, or dread accompanied by restlessness or tension.

Apathy: Lack of interest, concern, or emotion.

Aphasia: Difficulty understanding the speech of others and/or expressing oneself verbally.

Art Therapy: A form of therapy that allows people with dementia to express their feelings creatively through art.

Assessment: An evaluation, usually performed by a doctor, of a person's mental, emotional, and social capabilities.

Assisted-Living Facility: A residential care setting that combines housing, support services, and health care for people in the early or middle stages of a disabling disease, such as Alzheimer's disease.

Associated Disorders: Other medical or surgical conditions that are present, at the same time, which may or may not be contributing to the problem at-hand.

Asymptomatic: When there are no symptoms, or no clear sign, that disease is present.

Atrophy: Shrinking in size; often used to describe the loss of brain tissue seen during an autopsy of an Alzheimer's victim.

Autonomy: A person's ability to make independent choices.

Autopsy: The examination of a body's tissues and organs after death.

Behavioral Neurologist: A doctor who specializes in the diagnosis and treatment of behavioral and memory disorders that are due to brain disease.

Behavioral Symptoms: In Alzheimer's disease, emotional symptoms, such as wandering, depression, anxiety, hostility, and sleep disturbances.

Beneficiary: An individual, named in a will, who is designated to receive all or part of an estate, upon the death of the person who made the will.

Binswanger's disease: A type of dementia, associated with stroke-related changes in the brain.

Biomarker: Something used to indicate or measure a biological process, for example, levels of a specific protein in blood or spinal fluid. Detecting biomarkers specific to a disease can aid in the identification, diagnosis, and treatment of affected individuals, as well as people who may be at risk but who do not yet have symptoms.

Blood-Brain Barrier: The selective barrier that controls the entry of substances from the blood into the brain.

Blood Tests: A series of tests routinely done on blood to look for abnormalities associated with various diseases and conditions.

Brain: Along with the spinal cord, the brain makes up the central nervous system. It is the center of thought and emotion. It is responsible for the coordination and control of bodily activities and the interpretation of information from the senses.

Calcium: An element taken in through the diet that is essential for a variety of bodily functions, such as the communication between nerves, muscle contraction, and proper heart function. Imbalances in calcium can lead to many health problems and can cause nerve cell death.

Calcium Channel Blocker: A drug that blocks the entry of calcium into cells, thereby reducing activities that require calcium, such as nerve cell communication. Calcium channel blockers are used primarily in the treatment of certain heart conditions but are being studied as potential treatments for Alzheimer's disease.

Caregiver: The primary person in charge of caring for an individual with a serious illness, such as Alzheimer's disease; usually a family member or a designated health care professional.

Care Planning: A written action plan containing strategies for delivering care that addresses an individual's specific needs or problems.

Case Management: A term used to describe formal services planned by care professionals.

Cell: The fundamental unit of all organisms; the smallest structural unit capable of independent functioning.

Central Nervous System (CNS): One of the two major divisions of the nervous system. Composed of the brain and spinal cord, the CNS is the control network for the entire body.

Cerebral Cortex: The outer layer of the brain, consisting of nerve cells and the pathways that connect them. The cerebral cortex is the part of the brain in which thought processes take place. In Alzheimer's disease, nerve cells in the cerebral cortex degenerate and die.

Cerebrospinal Fluid (CSF): The fluid that fills the areas surrounding the brain and spinal cord.

Chest X-Ray (CXR; Chest Film): An image on film of the structures of the chest (heart, lungs, and bones); the procedure to get the image uses small amounts of radiation.

Choline: A natural substance required by the body that is obtained from various foods, such as eggs; an essential component of acetylcholine.

Choline Acetyltransferase (CAT): An enzyme that controls the production of acetylcholine. CAT appears to be depleted in the brains of individuals with Alzheimer's disease.

Cholinergic System: The system of nerve cells that uses acetylcholine to communicate between cells. It is damaged in the brains of individuals with Alzheimer's disease.

Cholinesterase: An enzyme that breaks down acetylcholine into active parts that can be recycled.

Chromosome: An H-shaped structure inside the cell nucleus, made up of tightly coiled strands of genes. Each chromosome is numbered (in humans: 1–46). Genes on chromosomes 1, 14, 19, and 21 are associated with Alzheimer's disease.

Clinical Psychologist: *See* Psychologist.

Clinical Social Worker: An individual who has specialized training in identifying and accessing community resources, such as: adult day care, home care, or nursing home services, as well as skills in individual and group counseling.

Glossary of Alzheimer's Disease Terms

Clinical Trial: An organized research program conducted with patients to evaluate a new medical treatment, drug, or device.

Co-existing Illness: A medical condition that exists simultaneously with another, such as arthritis and dementia.

Cognitive Abilities: Mental abilities, such as judgment, memory, learning, comprehension, and reasoning.

Cognitive Symptoms: In Alzheimer's disease, the symptoms that relate to loss of thought processes, such as learning, comprehension, memory, reasoning, and judgment.

Combativeness: Episodes of aggression.

Competence: A person's ability to make informed choices.

Computed (Axial) Tomography (CAT or CT) Scan: A technique in which multiple X-rays of the body are taken from different angles in a very short period of time. These images are collected by a computer, to give a series of images that look like slices of the body. In diagnosing dementia, CT scans can reveal tumors and small strokes in the brain.

Conservator: In some states, the guardian who manages an individual's assets.

Continuum of Care: Care services available to assist individuals throughout the course of a disease.

Controls: In a research trial, a group of people or animals that does not receive a treatment or other intervention or that is not affected by the disease being studied. This group is used as a standard to compare any changes in a group that receives treatment or has the disease. In Alzheimer's research, patients often are compared with controls of the same age (age-matched) to rule out the effects of age on study results.

Creutzfeldt-Jakob Disease: A rare disorder, of infectious and genetic origin, that typically causes memory failure and behavioral changes. A recently identified form is thought to be due to eating meat from cattle affected by mad cow disease.

CT Scan: *See* Computed (Axial) Tomography.

Deficits: Physical and/or cognitive skills or abilities that a person has lost, has difficulty with, or can no longer perform, because of his or her dementia.

Delusion: A false idea that is firmly believed and strongly maintained, in spite of contradictory proof or evidence.

Dementia: The loss of mental functions, such as thinking, memory, and reasoning, severe enough to interfere with a person's daily functioning. Dementia is not a disease itself, but rather a group of symptoms that may accompany certain diseases or conditions. Symptoms also may include changes in personality, mood, and behavior. Dementia is irreversible when caused by disease or injury, but may be reversible when caused by drugs, alcohol, hormone or vitamin imbalances, or depression.

Dementia-Capable: Skilled in working with people with dementia and their caregivers; knowledgeable about the kinds of services that may help them and aware of which agencies and individuals provide such services.

Dementia-Specific: Services that are provided specifically for people with dementia.

Depression: Low mood that prevents a person from leading a normal life and is associated with a variety of other symptoms.

Diagnosis: The process by which a doctor determines what disease a patient has by studying the patient's symptoms and medical history and analyzing results from any tests performed (blood tests, urine tests, brain scans, and so on).

Differential Diagnosis: The clinical evaluation of possible causes of dementia, to rule out all other factors before settling on Alzheimer's disease as a diagnosis.

Disorientation: A cognitive disability in which the person loses his/her sense of time, direction, and recognition.

DNA (Deoxyribonucleic Acid): The material that controls the genetics of each cell.

Double-Blind, Placebo-Controlled Study: A research procedure in which neither researchers nor patients know who is receiving the experimental substances or treatment and who is receiving a placebo.

Down Syndrome: A syndrome that causes slowed growth, abnormal facial features, and mental retardation. Down Syndrome is caused by an extra copy of all or part of chromosome 21. Most individuals with Down Syndrome develop Alzheimer's disease in adulthood.

Durable Power of Attorney: A legal document that allows an individual an opportunity to authorize another person, usually a trusted family member or friend, to make legal decisions when the person is no longer able to make legal decisions for him- or herself.

Durable Power of Attorney for Health Care: A legal document that allows an individual to appoint another person to make all decisions regarding health care, including choices regarding health care providers, medical treatment, and, in later stages of the disease, end-of-life decisions.

Dysphasia: The inability to find the right word, or understand the meaning of a word.

Early-Onset Alzheimer's Disease: An unusual form of Alzheimer's disease in which individuals are diagnosed with the disease before age sixty-five. Less than 10 percent of all Alzheimer's disease patients have early-onset disease. Early-onset Alzheimer's disease is sometimes associated with abnormalities in genes located on chromosomes 1, 14, and 21.

Early Stage: The beginning stages of Alzheimer's disease, when an individual experiences mild to moderate cognitive impairments.

Elder Law Attorney: An attorney who practices in the specialized area of law focusing on issues that typically affect older adults.

Electrocardiogram (ECG): A recording of the electrical activity of the heart.

Electroencephalogram (EEG): A procedure that measures the amount and type of brain wave activity, using electrodes placed on the surface of the scalp.

Environment: The physical and interpersonal surroundings that can affect mood and behavior in people with dementia.

Enzyme: A protein produced by living organisms that promotes or influences chemical reactions.

Estrogen: A sex hormone, produced by the ovaries and testes. Estrogen is also important for maintaining normal brain function and development of nerve cells.

Excitotoxicity: The overstimulation of nerve cells by nerves. Excitotoxicity often leads to cell damage or cell death.

Executor: The person named in a will who manages the estate of the deceased individual.

Familial Alzheimer's Disease: A form of Alzheimer's disease that runs in families.

Free-Standing, Dementia-Specific Care Center: A facility solely dedicated to the care of people with dementia. The facility can sometimes be part of a larger campus.

Functional Capabilities: What a person is able to do.

Gait: A person's manner of walking. People in the later stages of Alzheimer's disease often have a "reduced gait" which means their ability to lift their feet as they walk has diminished.

Gene: The basic unit of heredity found in all cells. Each gene occupies a certain location on a chromosome.

Genetic Counseling: A process in which a genetic counselor obtains a complete family and personal medical history, in order to determine the probable existence of a genetic problem occurring and recurring within a family.

Genetic Susceptibility: The state of being more likely than the average person to develop a disease as the result of genetics.

Genetic Testing: Certain tests that are ordered by a doctor who specializes in genetics, so that the presence of genetic abnormalities may be discovered. For patients and families suspected of having an inherited disease, it may be possible to find the mutation causing the disease through genetic testing of blood.

Genome: All the genes of an organism.

Geriatrician: A doctor who specializes in the medical care and treatment of older adults.

Glucose: A simple sugar that is a major energy source for all cellular and bodily functions. Glucose is obtained through the breakdown, or metabolism, of food in the digestive system.

Guardian: An individual appointed by the courts who is authorized to make legal and financial decisions for another person.

Hallucination: A sensory experience in which a person sees, hears, smells, tastes, or feels something that is not there.

Hippocampus: A part of the brain that is important for learning and memory.

Hoarding: Collecting and putting things away in order to guard them.

Hospice: The philosophy and approach to providing comfort and care rather than heroic life-saving measures at life's end.

Huntington's Disease: An inherited brain disease affecting the body that is characterized by mood changes, intellectual decline, and involuntary movement of limbs.

Immune System: The body's natural defense system against infection or disease; a system of cells that protects the body from bacteria, viruses, toxins, and other foreign substances.

Incontinence: Loss of bladder and/or bowel control.

Inflammatory Response: The immune system's normal response to tissue injury or abnormal stimulation caused by a physical, chemical, or biological substance.

Late-Onset Alzheimer's disease: The most common form of Alzheimer's disease, usually occurring after age sixty-five. Late-onset Alzheimer's disease affects almost half of all people over the age of eighty-five.

Late Stage: Designation given when dementia symptoms have progressed to the extent that a person has little capacity for self-care.

Lewy-Body Dementia: A dementing illness, associated with protein deposits called Lewy bodies, found in the cortex of the brain.

Living Trust: A legal document that allows an individual (the grantor or trustor) to create a trust and appoint someone else as trustee (usually a trusted individual or financial institution) to carefully invest and manage his or her assets.

Living Will: A legal document that expresses an individual's decision on the use of artificial life support systems.

Long-Term Care: A comprehensive range of medical, personal, and social services, coordinated to meet the physical, social, and emotional needs of people who are disabled or ill for extended periods of time.

Magnetic Resonance Imaging (MRI): A test that produces high-quality images of the body's internal structures, without the use of X-rays. MRI uses a large magnet, radio waves, and a computer to produce these images.

Medicaid: A program sponsored by the federal government and administered by states that is intended to provide health care and health-related services to low-income individuals.

Medicare: A federal health insurance program, for people age sixty-five and older and for individuals with disabilities.

Metabolism: The complex chemical and physical processes of living organisms that promote growth, sustain life, and enable other bodily functions to take place.

Mini-Mental State Examination: A standard mental status examination, routinely used to measure a person's basic cognitive skills, such as short-term memory, long-term memory, orientation, writing, and language.

MRI: *See* Magnetic Resonance Imaging.

Multi-Infarct Dementia (MID): A form of dementia also known as vascular dementia and caused by a number of strokes in the brain. These strokes can affect some intellectual abilities, impair movement and walking skills, and cause an individual to experience hallucinations, delusions, or depression. The onset of MID is usually abrupt and often progresses in a stepwise fashion. Individuals with MID are likely to have risk factors for strokes, such as high blood pressure, heart disease, or diabetes. MID cannot be treated; once nerve cells die, they cannot be replaced. However, risk factors can be treated, which may help prevent further damage.

Music Therapy: Use of music to improve physical, psychological, cognitive, and social functioning. *See also* Art Therapy.

Nerve Cell (Neuron): The basic working unit of the nervous system. Nerve cells send signals that control the actions of other cells in the body, such as other nerve cells and muscle cells.

Nerve Cell Transplantation: An experimental procedure in which normal brain cells are implanted into diseased areas of the brain, to replace dying or damaged cells.

Nerve Growth Factor (NGF): A protein that promotes nerve cell growth and may protect some types of nerve cells from damage.

Neuritic Plaque: *See* Amyloid Plaque.

Neurodegenerative disease: A type of neurological disorder marked by the loss of nerve cells. *See also* Alzheimer's Disease and Parkinson's Disease.

Neurofibrillary Tangle: An accumulation of twisted protein fragments inside nerve cells. Neurofibrillary tangles are one of the characteristic structural abnormalities found in the brains of people with Alzheimer's disease. The presence of amyloid plaques and neurofibrillary tangles, discovered at autopsy, is used to positively diagnose Alzheimer's disease.

Neurological Disorder: A disturbance in the structure or function of the nervous system resulting from developmental abnormality, disease, injury, or toxin.

Neurologist: A doctor who is specially trained to diagnose and treat disorders of the nervous system.

Neuron: *See* Nerve Cell (Neuron).

Neuropathology: Changes in the brain produced by a disease.

Neuropsychological testing: The evaluation of brain function and an individual's capabilities that uses tests to assess language, visual-perceptual skills, memory, attention, problem-solving, and reasoning.

Neuropsychologist: An individual who holds a doctoral degree (PhD or PsyD) in Clinical Psychology or a related discipline and who specializes in the evaluation and management of brain dysfunction.

Neurotransmission: The passage of signals from one nerve cell to another via chemical substances or electrical signals.

Neurotransmitter: A special chemical in the brain that is necessary for communication between nerve cells. Examples of neurotransmitters include acetylcholine, dopamine, norepinephrine, and serotonin.

Nucleus: The central component of a cell containing all genetic material.

Occupational Therapists: Health care professionals that teach people how to return to normal activities after injury or illness, using therapy and rehabilitation.

Onset: Defines the time when a disease begins, for example, early onset Alzheimer's; late-onset Alzheimer's.

Pacing: Aimless wandering or walking back and forth, often triggered by things like pain, hunger, or boredom, or by some distraction in the environment, such as noise, smell, or temperature.

Paranoia: Suspicion and fear of someone else that is not based on fact.

Glossary of Alzheimer's Disease Terms

Parkinson's Disease: A progressive, nervous-system disease, with an unknown cause, in which nerve cells in a specific area of the brain begin to die off. People with Parkinson's disease lack the neurotransmitter dopamine and have symptoms such as tremors, speech impairments, movement difficulties, and often, later in the course of the disease, dementia.

Peripheral Nervous System (PNS): One of the two major divisions of the nervous system. Nerves in the PNS, connect the central nervous system with sensory organs, other organs, muscles, blood vessels, and glands.

Personal Care: *See* Activities of Daily Living.

PET Scan: *See* Positron Emission Tomography (PET) Scan.

Pharmacology: The study of drugs, including their composition, production, uses, and effects in the body.

Pick's disease: A type of dementia, in which damage to nerve cells causes dramatic alterations in personality and social behavior but typically does not affect memory until later in the disease.

Pillaging: Taking things that belong to someone else. A person with dementia may think something belongs to him or her even when it clearly does not.

Placebo: An inactive material that looks the same as an active drug; for example, a sugar pill. *See also* Double-Blind, Placebo-Controlled Study.

Plaques and Tangles: *See* Amyloid Plaque and Neurofibrillary Tangle.

Positron Emission Tomography (PET) Scan: An imaging scan, that measures brain function.

Possible Alzheimer's Disease: A suspicion of Alzheimer's disease based on the patient's medical history and the results of neurological, psychiatric, and clinical exams, neuropsychological tests, and laboratory studies.

Premature Aging: Physical changes related to aging that occur ahead of what would be expected for a person's chronological age.

Presenilins: Proteins that may be linked to early-onset Alzheimer's disease.

Principal: The individual signing the power of attorney to authorize another person to legally make decisions for him or her.

Prions: Protein segments that may cause infection and may lead to some forms of dementia.

Probable Alzheimer's Disease: A relative certainty that the diagnosis is Alzheimer's disease based on the progressive deterioration of specific cognitive functions, motor skills, and perception, impaired activities of daily living, and altered patterns of behavior, in addition to family history and laboratory findings.

Prognosis: The probable outcome or course of a disease; the chance of recovery.

Progressive Disorder: A disorder that gets worse over time.

Pseudo-Dementia: A severe form of depression, resulting from a progressive brain disorder in which cognitive changes mimic those of dementia.

Psychiatrist: Medical doctor (MD or DO) who specializes in treating mental, emotional, or behavioral disorders. Psychiatrists can prescribe medications, in addition to performing psychotherapy.

Psychologist: Psychology professional who is not a medical doctor and cannot prescribe medication but does perform evaluations and use psychotherapy. Psychologists usually have advanced degrees (PhD or PsyD) and receive additional training to work with patients. They are also referred to as clinical psychologists.

Special-Care Unit: A designated area of a residential care facility or nursing home, that cares specifically for the needs of people with Alzheimer's disease.

Spinal Cord: One of the two components of the central nervous system. The spinal cord is the main relay for signals between the brain and the rest of the body.

Stages: The course of disease progression, defined by levels or periods of severity: early, mild, moderate, moderately severe, severe.

Sundowning: Unsettled behavior evident in the late afternoon or early evening.

Support Group: A facilitated gathering of patients, caregivers, family, friends, or others affected by a disease or condition, for the purpose of discussing issues related to the disease.

Suspiciousness: A mistrust common in Alzheimer's patients, as their memory becomes progressively worse. An example is when patients believe their belongings have been stolen, because they have forgotten where they left them.

Synapse: The junction where a signal is transmitted from one nerve cell to another, usually by a neurotransmitter.

Tangle: *See* Neurofibrillary Tangle.

Tissue: A group of similar cells that act together in the performance of a particular function.

Toxin: A substance that can cause illness, injury, or death; produced by living organisms.

Trigger: An environmental or personal stimulus that sets off a particular behavior.

Trustee: The individual or financial institution managing the assets of a living trust.

Urinalysis: A test in which a urine sample is evaluated to detect abnormalities.

Vitamins: Various substances found in plants and animals that are required for life-sustaining processes.

Acknowledgments

I want to thank my special friends who have helped me make this book possible:

Julia Cheung, Esq., whose interest was motivated by seeing her grandfather struggle with Alzheimer's disease. Julia researched and wrote the chapters concerning legal, financial, and elder abuse.

Barbara Eubanks was a diligent researcher who combed through mountains of articles and books to see that our information was current and accurate.

Marjorie Elliott was a resourceful organizer of content, grammar, and endless editing.

Phyllis Salerno makes my life manageable and has reread and reread to assure that this book is easily readable to all who are interested in this disease that touches so many lives.

About the Author

Bettye Martin Musham is a graduate of Duke University School of Nursing and serves on its advisory board. She co-founded the Duke Islamic Study Center and serves on its board as well. Her career spans many creative positions, and she has served on multiple corporations' boards of directors. She resides in Bucks County, Pennsylvania, and New York City.

www.ingramcontent.com/pod-product-compliance
Lightning Source LLC
Chambersburg PA
CBHW071204160426
43196CB00011B/2195